Morningside Center for Teaching Social Responsibility

THE 4Rs™ TEACHING GUIDE 5

Reading, Writing, Respect & Resolution

Maxine Phillips & Tom Roderick

The 4Rs™ (Reading, Writing, Respect & Resolution)
A Teaching Guide, Grade 5
Principal Writers: Maxine Phillips & Tom Roderick
Literacy Consultant: Barbara Danish
Editing & Design: Leslie Dennis

New edition
Copyright © 2015 by Morningside Center for Teaching Social Responsibility; prior editions 2012, 2007
All rights reserved.
Educators have permission to copy handouts for classroom use.

ISBN-13: 978-1-931630-75-7
ISBN-13: 978-1-931630-15-3 (Learning Kit / Grade 5)

Published by Morningside Center for Teaching Social Responsibility
475 Riverside Drive, Suite 550, New York, NY 10115
T: 212 870 3318 x38 / F: 212 870 2464
Website: www.morningsidecenter.org / Email: LDennis@morningsidecenter.org

Acknowledgments

The 4Rs has been the work of many hands, minds, and hearts. We first express our gratitude to the following people, organizations, agencies, and institutions that helped us create and launch The 4Rs:

- The working group of teachers from New York City's Community School District 15 who, in a series of meetings during the 1998-99 school year, helped us decide on the themes the curriculum would address and develop an overall plan: Sara Barnes, Paula Beck, Mary Ellen Bosch, Sheila Brooks, Bea Byrd, Alexa Fila, Christina Fuentes, Millie Fulford, Beth Handman, Linda Harris, Catherine Kelly, Lorrie Mann, and Joel Moss.

- The teachers who piloted the draft units during the 1999-2000 school year and gave us their feedback: Chris Bellman, Alison Brackman, Susan Butler, Sarah Button, Alev Dervish, Eileen Eiger, Linda Harris, Julio Jimenez, Cathy Kelly, Lorrie Mann, Denise McCarthy, Joel Moss, Ellen Neipris, Mary Beth Palmer, Donna Pasquariello, Pascale Pradel, Debra Sit, and Kim Tulloch.

- Frank DeStefano, Superintendent of CSD 15, and Wilfredo Laboy, Assistant Superintendent, who supported the project from the beginning and made it possible for teachers to participate.

- Principals of the schools where teachers piloted the units: Mary Manti, Principal, P.S. 15; Yvette Aguirre, Principal, P.S. 24; Linda Leff, Principal, P.S. 58; Josephine Santiago, Principal, P.S. 169; Howard Wholl, Principal, P.S. 230; Judi Aronson, Principal, P.S. 261; Liz Phillips, Principal, P.S. 321.

- Morningside Center (then called Educators for Social Responsibility Metropolitan Area/ESR Metro) staff members: Barbara Barnes, Lillian Castro, Leslie Dennis, Larry Garvin, Laura McClure, Nino Nannarone, Mary Schreiber, Heather Smith, and Jeanette Toomer.

- Barbara Danish, our literacy consultant, who emphasized the importance of writing as a tool for thinking.

- People whose work in the field of conflict resolution/social and emotional learning contributed to our thinking about the 4Rs: Sheila Alson, Larry Dieringer, William Kreidler, Linda Lantieri, Priscilla Prutzman, Jinnie Spiegler, Sandy Whittal, and the staff of the New York City Board of Education Office of the Resolving Conflict Creatively Program: Donna Connelly, Mariana Gaston, Ellen Icolari, Hannah Kirschner, Angela Morgan, Debra Schaller-Demers, Lina Sullivan, Jim Tobin, Manny Verdi.

- Our Foundation and Corporate Supporters: Booth Ferris Foundation, Chase Bank, Fund for the City of New York, J.P. Morgan Charitable Trust, Met Life Foundation, Overbrook Foundation, The Philip and Lynn Straus Foundation, The Pinkerton Foundation.

Second, we thank the following people, organizations, agencies, and institutions that, believing in The 4Rs, have helped us develop, sustain, and expand the program:

- The thousands of teachers who have studied the teaching guides and taught the curriculum to their students.
- Principals who have championed The 4Rs in their schools and beyond, especially Christina Fuentes, P.S. 24, Brooklyn; David Cintron, P.S. 214, The Bronx; Lisa Manfredonia, P.S. 62, The Bronx; Maria Nunziata, P.S. 130, Brooklyn: Roberta Davenport, P.S. 307, Brooklyn; and Rose Dubitsky, P.S 24, Brooklyn.
- Jenni Turner, early childhood teacher, who advised us in writing The 4Rs Teaching Guide for Pre-k.

- Audrey Major and Janice Marie Johnson, Morningside Center staff members, who helped shape The 4Rs for Middle School.
- Jill Merolla, Supervisor of Community Outreach and Grant Development for the Warren City Schools, who championed The 4Rs, a key component of Warren's SEL Skills for Life Program.
- The research team that conducted the gold-standard (randomized control) study of The 4Rs Program: Dr. J. Lawrence Aber, New York University, Dr. Joshua Brown, Fordham University, and Dr. Stephanie Jones, Harvard University.
- The research team for Goal 2 4Rs+My Teaching Partner (MTP) Project: Dr. Joshua Brown, Fordham University; Drs. Jason Downer and Megan Stuhlman, University of Virginia; Dr. Stephanie Jones, Harvard University.
- The research team for the federally funded Goal 3 randomized control trial of the 4Rs + My Teaching Partner Project: Dr. Joshua Brown, Fordham University; and Drs. Jason Downer and Megan Stuhlman, University of Virginia.
- Suzanne Bouffard, who wrote a great article about The 4Rs-MTP Project for the New York Tiimes.
- Our friends at the Collaborative for Academic, Social, and Emotional Learning (CASEL), especially Roger Weissberg and the late Mary Utne O'Brien.
- My dear long-time colleague Linda Lantieri, Director, Inner Resilience Program, from whom we have learned much that has strengthened all of Morningside Center's work, including The 4Rs.
- Susan Fountain, who is helping us highlight and strengthen the aspects of The 4Rs that helps students pause, focus, and pay attention to what is happening in the present moment.
- Those of our staff developers who have trained and coached teachers in The 4Rs: Audrey Major, Ava Daniel, Mariana Gaston, Emma Gonzalez, Janice Marie Johnson, Javier Diaz, Joseph McCarthy, Joyce Griffen, Kristin Page Stuart, Marieke van Woerkom,
- Carolina Kroon, photographer and videographer, who captured many images and videos of 4Rs activities over the years.
- Leslie Dennis, Morningside Center Program Associate, who designed The 4Rs Teaching Guides and Learning Kits and handles production and shipping of the guides and kits with loving and much appreciated attention to detail.
- The authors and illustrators of the wonderful children's books that introduce The 4Rs units.
- Connie Cuttle who has championed Morningside Center's work, including The 4Rs, as Director of Professional Development, the Office of Safety and Youth Development, New York City Department of Education.
- Our funders: Jean and Louis Dreyfus Foundation, Keith and Miller Foundation, Marianne Montero, New York City Department of Education, New York Community Trust, Novo Foundation, Philip and Lynn Straus Foundation, The Pinkerton Foundation, Tiger Foundation, U.S. Department of Education, U.S. Department of Education, Institute of Education Sciences, WT Grant Foundation.
- Maxine Phillips, my wife and co-author, whose appreciation for high-quality children's literature and her knack for finding just the right book to launch each unit have immeasurably enriched The 4Rs.

Tom Roderick
Executive Director
Morningside Center for Teaching Social Responsibility
August 2015

Contents

Introduction

Welcome to The 4Rs!

You are about to embark on an adventure with your students than can transform your classroom, their lives, and perhaps your own. The 4Rs™ (Reading, Writing, Respect, and Resolution) is a unique program that combines excellent children's literature with social and emotional skill-building. Research has shown that when it is adopted school wide it has measurable impact on both classroom atmosphere and students' social, emotional, and cognitive development. As students learn the skills they need to deal constructively with their peers and to manage their own emotions, they are able to focus more easily on academics.

A program of Morningside Center for Teaching Social Responsibility, The 4Rs integrates social and emotional learning (SEL) and language arts from pre-kindergarten to 8th grade. Through the program, Morningside Center provides training and classroom coaching to prepare teachers to teach weekly lessons based on The 4Rs curriculum.

The 4Rs for pre-k to 5th grade uses high-quality children's literature and engaging interactive activities to develop students' skills and understanding in seven areas: building community, understanding and handling feelings, listening, assertiveness, problem-solving, dealing well with diversity, and cooperation. The 4Rs curriculum is grade-specific: Each grade has its own teaching guide, books, and age-appropriate activities.

Each 4Rs unit begins with a Read-aloud of a children's book, carefully chosen for its high literary quality and relevance to the theme. Next is Book Talk — discussion, writing, and role-play to deepen students' understanding of the book and connect it to their lives. Then comes Applied Learning — skills practice related to the theme.

By highlighting universal themes of feelings, relationships, conflict, and community, the 4Rs curriculum adds meaning and depth to literacy instruction. Since reading and writing are excellent tools for exploring social and emotion themes, The 4Rs enriches SEL instruction as well.

The 4Rs engages parents through "4Rs Family Connections," which has two parts:
- activities children do at home with their parents and

- workshops that bring parents together to explore how social and emotional skills can strengthen their relationships with their children.

The 4Rs program has been rigorously studied, thanks to a grant from the U. S. Department of Education.[1] A gold-standard study by top researchers at New York University and Fordham University tracked the development of children in nine New York City elementary schools that implemented the program compared with the development of children in nine control schools. Compared with children in the control schools, children in the 4Rs schools were less hyperactive, less aggressive, and saw their social world as less hostile. They showed fewer symptoms of depression and were more likely to resolve interpersonal problems competently.

What's more, during the first year children judged to be at greatest behavioral risk by their teachers had better attendance than their counterparts in the control schools and made better academic progress as rated by teachers. By the second year, they were also doing better on standardized tests.

At the end of the first year, independent ("blind") observers assessed the quality of classroom climate in all third-grade classrooms in the 18 schools using a research-based observational instrument called the Classroom Assessment Scoring System (CLASS). These observations showed significantly higher levels of overall classroom quality among classrooms in the 4Rs schools compared to classrooms in the control schools. Specifically, classrooms in 4Rs schools had significantly higher levels of emotional and instructional support compared to classrooms in control schools. Other research has shown a strong correlation between higher levels on the CLASS and more positive social and emotional development and higher academic achievement.

The 4Rs is closely aligned with the national standards set by CASEL (Collaborative for Academic, Social, and Emotional Learning): The 4Rs Program received CASEL's highest ratings in its Guide to Effective SEL Programs (pre-k-5). The 4Rs is also included in the federal Substance Abuse and Mental Health Services Administration's National Registry of Evidence-Based Programs and Practices.

Taken together, the ratings and research above demonstrate that The 4Rs Program is an evidence-based program that should be available to schools everywhere.

---

[1] Jones, S. M., Brown, J. L.& Aber, J. L. (2011). Two-year impacts of a universal school-based social-emotional and literacy intervention: An experiment in translational developmental research. *Child Development*, 82 (2), 533–554.

Social and Emotional Learning

Morningside Center defines social and emotional learning (SEL) as the process by which we develop our capacity to understand and manage our feelings, relate well to others, deal well with conflict and other life challenges, make good decisions, and take responsibility for improving our communities – from the classroom to the world.

Each of these competencies is made up of a number of skills. For example, **_Understanding and managing our feelings_** involves, among other things, the ability to be aware of and name our feelings, an understanding of the physical cues to emotions, insight into what triggers certain emotions, and the ability to express emotions appropriately and constructively.

The ability to relate well to others requires the ability to read the emotions of others, empathize, listen actively, and communicate assertively. It also includes the capacity to understand similarities and differences; to work respectfully across gender, race, ethnic, religious, economic, ability, and other types of differences; and to examine one's own assumptions and stereotypes.

Dealing well with conflict and other life challenges involves emotional self-management, effective listening and communication skills, and an understanding that what one asks for in conflict and what one really needs may not be the same. It also includes the ability to come up with alternative solutions to conflicts, skill in evaluating possible solutions, and a commitment to solving problems in a way that meets the real needs of all parties.

Making good decisions requires awareness of the motivations behind our choices; engages students' ability to assess the consequences of those choices; encourages students to think about how decisions they take will affect them, others, and the larger community; and helps students look back at decisions made and assess their impact.

Taking responsibility for improving our communities harnesses the skills described above in the service of social justice. It entails an understanding of what justice means and the ability to identify situations of injustice, as well as familiarity with the actions of those who have made a difference in our society. It also requires that students see themselves as capable of taking responsible action and are willing to take meaningful action, both individually and with others.

Taking time to slow down and focus on these skills is something that may be new to your students. Yet the ability to step back and notice our feelings and thoughts, as well as how we are interacting with others, is foundational to developing and using social and emotional competencies. Throughout the 4Rs curriculum, there are activities that help students to pay attention to their sensory experiences, thoughts, and emotions in the present moment. These activities may

---

The seven units in The 4Rs are designed to support the development of these SEL competencies:

Unit 1, Community Building, helps students build a sense of caring and connection in their classrooms.

Unit 2, Feelings, heightens students' awareness of their own emotions, and those of others, while providing practical strategies for managing strong emotions like anger.

Unit 3, Listening, fosters skills that enable students to understand where others are coming from, learn from them, and empathize with them.

Unit 4, Assertiveness, is about being strong but not mean in expressing one's needs and in standing up for what one thinks is right

Unit 5: Problem Solving, shows how to resolve issues and handle conflicts in ways that meet the priority needs of both parties.

Unit 6, Diversity, cultivates a sense of one's own identity, respect for differences, and commitment to standing up to bullying.

Unit 7, Making a Difference, looks how others have brought about change, with the goal of creating positive change in the classroom, school, local community, and beyond.

involve simply noticing their breathing, attending to sounds, or being more aware of their physical movements. Building this kind of awareness encourages students to pause, notice what is happening inside and outside themselves, and respond thoughtfully rather than react automatically. Research suggests that when these types of activities are used regularly, they may help students feel more centered, manage their emotions more effectively, and increase both attention and social-emotional competency.[2]

The impact of SEL programs

In schools where SEL is well-implemented, students develop their social and emotional competencies; become partners with adults in creating vibrant learning communities; and learn to care about and respect other people, including those who are different or who live far away.

A growing body of research shows that students in high quality SEL programs
- show improved social and emotional skills and behavior;
- decrease their classroom misbehavior and aggression;
- increase positive attitudes about themselves, others and school;
- improve their attendance
- reduce their anxiety and depression;
- are less like to be suspended;
- gain in achievement test scores and have better grades.

A new vision for education

Morningside Center understands SEL as a set of attitudes, practices, and policies that are fully integrated into the life and culture of the school, rather than as an add-on "program." SEL can provide a rich vision of education and a basis for reflecting on everything that goes on in a school. By asking how school policies and practices are affecting students' social and emotional development, SEL can be a powerful lever for school improvement. By building caring and connections, SEL also lays a solid foundation for social responsibility, not only toward friends and family but toward ever-widening circles of community.

---

[2] Greenberg, M. T. & Harris, A. R. (2012). Nurturing mindfulness in children and youth: Current state of research. *Child Development Perspectives, 6* (2), 161-166.

Morningside Center for Teaching Social Responsibility

Morningside Center works hand in hand with educators to help young people develop the values, personal qualities, and skills they need to thrive and contribute to their communities—from the classroom to the world.

Since our founding in 1982, Morningside Center has developed an array of programs to engage young people in learning essential social and emotional skills and to support educators in making their schools productive and respectful. Over the years our programs have reached hundreds of schools, tens of thousands of educators, and hundreds of thousands of students, grades pre-k - 12, in New York City and beyond.

Major scientific studies have found that our programs have a significant positive impact on students' behavior, their social and emotional competency, their academic performance, and on the classroom climate for learning. The Collaborative for Academic, Social & Emotional Learning (CASEL) has selected two of our programs (The 4Rs and Resolving Conflict Creatively) as among the nation's top 23 SEL programs.

We are part of a nationwide movement to make high-quality, research-validated social and emotional learning an integral part of every child's education.

For more information visit our website at www.morningsidecenter.org.

Tom Roderick
Executive Director
August 2015

Tips for Teachers: Getting the most from The 4Rs™

1. **Do at least one lesson a week throughout the school year.** Consistency is the key to effectiveness. This means making The 4Rs a priority, not an optional activity you do if time permits. It means continuing to teach The 4Rs even when standardized tests are looming. In fact, you can use 4Rs ideas and skills to help your students handle their feelings about the tests and lower their stress level so that they can improve their performance.

2. **Choose prime time at the same time each week for your 4Rs lessons.** Your week will go better if your 4Rs lesson is first thing Monday morning (or Tuesday morning if Monday is a holiday). Avoid Friday afternoons! In fact, The 4Rs is most successful when all classroom teachers are teaching The 4Rs at the same time each week. During that time, the entire staff of the school is doing 4Rs, with out-of-classroom staff (guidance counselors and social workers, for example) assisting classroom teachers and principals and assistant principals visiting classrooms to observe and publicly acknowledge good work by students and teachers.

3. **Spend about five weeks per unit.** Because there are seven units, it will take about 35 weeks to teach the entire curriculum. Each unit consists of a Read-aloud, Book Talk, and (with a few exceptions) three Applied Learning lessons in the workshop format (see below). Do the Read-aloud and Book Talk in Week 1 and the Applied Learning lessons in Weeks 2, 3, and 4. Use Week 5 to engage the students in a project related to the unit, to reinforce a skill with which the students need more practice, to revisit the Read-aloud for the unit, and/or read them another book on the theme.

4. **Meet weekly with colleagues to share experiences and ideas** and do problem solving when challenges arise. At a minimum The 4Rs should be on the agenda of grade meetings each week. In addition, interested teachers may want to set up a weekly conversation about the curriculum over lunch.

5. **Teach the curriculum in the sequence provided.** Dealing well with feelings, being a good listener, and being assertive (strong, not mean) lay the foundation for effective problem solving, for cultural sharing and standing up to bullying, and for making a difference. Of course, if a teachable moment arises, you can take the opportunity to bring in an idea or skill from a later or earlier unit. But keep your main focus on the unit at hand.

6. **Use the workshop format for the Applied Learning lessons.** The lessons are carefully designed to provide an optimal context for learning. The full lesson or workshop has a much greater impact than doing the activities out-of- context.

The <u>Gathering</u> helps students leave behind any baggage they're carrying from other parts of their day and directs their attention to "4Rs Time." <u>Checking the Agenda</u> gives students some ownership over this part of their day. The core activities address the workshop's key objectives. The <u>Evaluation</u> gives you feedback on students' perceptions of the lesson. The <u>Closing</u> ends the workshop on a positive note and gives the message that "4Rs Time" is over for the day.

7. **Call the time you set aside for 4Rs instruction "4Rs Time."** Make sure students know what the 4Rs stand for. Of course, as The 4Rs takes root in your classroom, you'll be applying 4Rs ideas and skills throughout the day. But it's important that "4Rs Time" has its own identity as a special time to focus attention on social and emotional learning — in the same way that reading goes on throughout the day but there's the "literacy block" when attention is focused on literacy.

8. **"4Rs Time" works best when the students sit in a circle.** Have the students sit in a circle on the rug. Or, if the students will be sitting in chairs, have them move furniture and arrange their chairs, as necessary. You can turn this task into a cooperative game by asking them to do this in silence and as quickly as possible. Time them and post the result, and next time see if they beat their best time so far.

9. **Use a talking piece — with discretion.** Morningside Center recommends using a talking piece as part of a structured "circle" process for fostering deep communication when you want everyone's voice to be heard by everyone else in your class. The students are sitting in a circle with no obstructions in the middle. The talking piece is passed around the circle in order from one student to the next. In this way, each member of the circle is invited to speak, and they know when their turn is coming up. They can pass if they want to. When a student is holding the talking piece, it's that student's turn to talk and enjoy the full attention of the group. No one is allowed to go out of turn — to interrupt, ask a question, or make a comment. All have to wait until the talking piece comes around to them. You don't have time to go through this process for everything you want your students to share. For brainstorming, a brief discussion, or calling on a couple of students to speak after a pair-share, a talking piece might be cumbersome. Feel free to integrate a circle with talking piece into The 4Rs when you want to slow things down a bit and take the time to hear everybody's thinking.

10. **Foster SEL all day every day by**
    - modeling the skills you are teaching your students
    - integrating 4Rs ideas, skills, and activities into other areas of the curriculum
    - taking advantage of teachable moments, and

- engaging your students in special projects (for example, creating posters on SEL themes to display around the school or creating skits to perform for other classes or for parents).

11. **Model active listening with your students.** Your teaching of The 4Rs curriculum will be most successful if students feel comfortable sharing their experiences and their thinking. Listen without judgment, use active listening techniques (like paraphrasing) to draw out their thinking, and encourage them to share their points of view with you and each other in respectful ways. If you feel the need to challenge a student's ideas or correct misinformation, do so gently and respectfully and, as much as possible, by asking questions that complicate the student's thinking.

12. **Set aside a few minutes each day for silence.** The school day is hectic and stressful for students and teachers. It's useful to build in time each day for a few minutes of silence. During this time the lights are off. No writing, drawing, or reading. Just sitting. Ask students to put their hands on their knees. They can close their eyes if they want. Tell them that they can let their minds use the silence as they wish. Or you can suggest ways they might use the silence. For example,

    - practice abdominal breathing (introduced in Unit 2)
    - simply pay attention to your breathing
    - pay attention to sounds you hear
    - in your mind, take yourself to a peaceful place
    - recall a time you had fun
    - recall something you like to do

    a. After the time of silence, ask for a couple of volunteers to share where their minds went during the time. Make time for silence each day at the same time. You might carve out a few minutes for silence when the students come back from lunch and recess and/or at the beginning of the day. Throughout the curriculum we suggest times when teachers might ask students to pause and pay attention to what is happening inside (their sensations, images, feelings, thoughts) and outside (sounds, sights, the feelings and behavior of others). The ability to pause and pay attention to what's happening in the moment is a key social and emotional skill that promotes self-awareness and self-management.

    b. A few minutes of silence at strategic times during the day will pay off in a calmer, more focused class. And you'll be developing in your students a habit and skill that will serve them well throughout their lives.

    c. Be sure to take this opportunity to enjoy a couple of minutes of silence yourself!

13. **Consider having your students keep a 4Rs/SEL journal.** Writing (drawing for younger students) is an excellent way to reinforce and consolidate learning. A powerful research-based study technique is to follow the reading of a text by writing about it, perhaps summarizing the main points of an argument and articulating your response. By writing about a text we can test our understanding and identify gaps we can fill by reviewing sections of the text. We enhance our memory of the text. And we exercise our creative- thinking muscles as we fashion our response. That's why we've included writing exercises as part of Book Talk in all units for all grades. A journal enables students to put all of their Book Talk writing in one place. You can also give them a few minutes after each 4Rs lesson to jot down a few thoughts about what they're taking away or how they're planning to use what they've just learned. If a student tries a new skill, s/he might want to write about what happened. Did it bring a positive result? If a student is stuck in a conflict with someone, s/he might want to do some writing to sort it out and imagine some solutions. You can give your students standard journals and encourage them to decorate them. By having students keep journals, you will be introducing them to a habit or practice that can serve them well the rest of their lives.

14. **Class meetings for problem solving are an excellent extension of The 4Rs.** In this kind of class meeting the teacher empowers students, facilitating a process by which they apply the skills they're developing through 4Rs lessons to real-life problems in classroom and school. Introduce class meetings for problem solving after completing Unit 5. By this time your students will have the foundational skills (managing feelings, listening, assertiveness) to be good problem solvers. Also, Unit 5 has a lesson on the ABCDE problem-solving model, an approach that children can easily grasp. A free downloadable copy of Morningside Center's comprehensive guide, *Class Meetings for Problem Solving*, is available by request.

15. **Add your own ideas.** You know your students. Tailor the curriculum to their needs and interests and add your own creative ideas. We've described the recommended activities fully to get you started, but The 4Rs is not a scripted curriculum. Once you get the hang of it, you'll see additional ways to enhance the students' understanding of key ideas and strengthen their skills. Be creative and share your ideas and experiences with your colleagues.

16. **Hang in there, even when the going gets tough.** This is hard work; it can also be immensely gratifying. Gandhi thought of his life as a series of "experiments in nonviolence." He tried things—some worked, some didn't. He learned from his mistakes, kept trying and ended up making a huge difference. In similar fashion, "4Rs Time" provides a great opportunity for you to make a huge difference in the lives of your students.

The 4Rs
Overview of Themes & Books

UNIT	Pre-K	Kindergarten	1st Grade	2nd Grade
Unit 1: Building community	*Hurry, Hurry* by Eve Bunting	*Subway Sparrow* by Leyla Torres	*The Doorbell Rang* by Pat Hutchins	*The Big Orange Splot* by Daniel Manus Pinkwater
Unit 2: Feelings	*Glad Monster, Sad Monster, A Book About Feelings* by Ed Emberley and Anne Miranda	*Mama, Do You Love Me?* by Barbara Joosse <u>Alternate:</u> *When Sophie Gets Angry, Really, Really Angry* by Mollie Bang	*Chrysanthemum* by Kevin Henkes	*We Are Best Friends* by Aliki
Unit 3: Listening	*The Listening Walk* by Paul Showers	*The Hating Book* by Charlotte Zolotow	*Max Found Two Sticks*, written and illustrated by Brian Pinkney	*Angel Child, Dragon Child* by Michele Maria Surat
Unit 4: Assertiveness	*Don't let the Pigeon Drive the Bus* by Mo Willem	*George and Martha: One Fine Day* and *George and Martha: Tons of Fun* by James Marshall	*Daisy Comes Home* by Jan Brett	*The Recess Queen* by Alexis O'Neill, illus. by Laura Huliska-Beith
Unit 5: Problem solving	*The Knight and the Dragon* by Tomie dePaola	*Zinnia and Dot* by Lisa Campbell Ernst	*Owen* by Kevin Henkes	*Luka's Quilt* by Georgia Guback
Unit 6: Diversity	*The Foot Book* by Dr. Seuss	*Stellaluna* by Janell Cannon	*The Ugly Vegetables* by Grace Lin	*Crow Boy* by Taro Yashima
Unit 7: Making a difference	*Click, Clack, MOO, Cows that Type* by Doreen Cronin	*Swimmy* by Leo Lionni	*The Bremen Town Musicians* / retold and illustrated by Ilse Plume	*Wangari's Trees of Peace* by Jeanette Winter

The 4Rs

Overview of Themes & Books

UNIT	3rd Grade	4th Grade	5th Grade
Unit 1: Building community	*Stone Soup* by Marcia Brown	*Alejandro's Gift* by Richard E. Albert	*The Keeping Quilt* by Patricia Polacco
Unit 2: Feelings	*JoJo's Flying Side Kick* by Brian Pinkney	*Sarah, Plain and Tall* by Patricia MacLachlan	*Mysterious Traveler* by Mal Peet & Elspeth Graham (authors), P.J. Lynch (illustrator)
Unit 3: Listening	*The Pain and the Great One* by Judy Blume	*The Other Way to Listen* by Byrd Baylor and Peter Parnall	*Encounter* by Jane Yolen
Unit 4: Assertiveness	*Hank Aaron: Brave in Every Way* by Peter Golenbock	*The Story of Ruby Bridges* by Robert Coles	*Your Move* by Eve Bunting
Unit 5: Problem solving	*Old Henry* by Joan W. Blos	*Chandra's Magic Light: A Story in Nepal,* by Theresa Heine; Judith Gueyfier (illustrator)	*Brothers in Hope* by Mary Williams & R. Gregory Christie
Unit 6: Diversity	*One* by Kathryn Otoshi	*The Hundred Dresses* by Eleanor Estes	*Friends from the Other Side* by Gloria Anzaldua
Unit 7: Making a difference	*Baseball Saved Us* by Ken Mochizuki	*Moses: When Harriet Tubman Led Her People to Freedom* by Carole Boston Weatherford	*Sweet Clara and the Freedom Quilt* by Deborah Hopkinson

5

Unit I Theme

Building Community: Developing a Vision

Unit I Book Selection

The Keeping Quilt by Patricia Polacco
Simon and Schuster, 1988.

Activities

- Deeping our Understanding of Community
- Making a Classroom Quilt: Envisioning a Caring Community
- Good and Poor Listening
- Think Differently
- Put-ups and Put-downs
- Have a Heart with Heart Story
- Additional Activities

Introduction

Human beings are social and interdependent. We live in and interact with many, many groups, such as family, neighborhood, school, city, state, country, planet, or groups based on faith, work, play, and common identities or interests. However, being part of a group that shares similar characteristics does not necessarily mean that one is part of a community as we use the term here. By community, we mean connection, caring, and solidarity. Such communities do not just happen. They are the result of shared vision and conscious effort. Martin Luther King, Jr. spoke of a dream, of a "beloved community." He articulated a vision that many people share. We all deserve to be part of communities that are safe, fair, caring, respectful, appreciative, and nurturing of our talents. When we speak of building a classroom community, we are talking about creating a group that has those qualities.

Teachers build community through their approach to classroom management. That's the bedrock upon which all else rests. Community building can also occur through the study of literature, which presents visions of community; through discussions in which students and teachers discuss, disagree, and come to various understandings in a supportive context; and through conscious decisions about rights and responsibilities as members of the community.

The dominant U.S. culture is one of the most individualistic in the world. There is a constant

> **Community Building in the Classroom Involves**
>
> - **creating a vision of the community you want and setting goals**
>
> - **establishing concrete rules & expectations**
>
> - **enforcing consequences when rules are not followed or expectations not met**
>
> - **establishing and observing group rituals**
>
> - **developing individuals' self-control and interpersonal skills**
>
> - **ongoing communication and problem solving**
>
> - **regular class meetings**

tension in our society between the rights of individuals and the rights of groups. These tensions are played out in everyday life as well as in legislatures and courts of law (think of compulsory education, home-schooling, and the right of the Amish to withdraw their children from school at age 14). Existing within the dominant culture are cultures of immigrant and indigenous groups that place more emphasis on community than on individual expression. Literature about different groups will reflect such attitudes and conflicts. Classroom discussion can range over a variety of issues, such as the balance between group rights and individual rights; the oppressiveness of small communities in which everyone knows everybody's business vs. the intimacy of small communities in which everyone cares about each other; the roles people play in communities; the need for leadership in building community; the variety of communities; and the different assumptions or principles that hold communities together.

At the beginning of the school year, teachers usually spend time establishing class rules and routines. This unit intends to support that process. We can think of class rules as guidelines for creating classroom community. The teacher provides good leadership for the community, but guidelines are most effective when developed with the participation of the group.

In this unit students will work with the literature to exercise their imaginations. They will develop their visions of community, learn to listen to each other, and learn to apply the literature to the ongoing process of building community in their classrooms and the world beyond.

<table>
<tr><td colspan="2">Rules for a Classroom Community Might Include</td></tr>
<tr><td>•</td><td>listening well</td></tr>
<tr><td>•</td><td>tolerating disagreements and diverse points of view</td></tr>
<tr><td>•</td><td>respecting each other's bodies</td></tr>
<tr><td>•</td><td>respecting each other's property</td></tr>
<tr><td>•</td><td>respecting each other's feelings</td></tr>
</table>

In this unit

	Ideas	Skills
Literacy	• Unifying theme • Symbolism	• Identifying the main idea • Predicting
Social and Emotional Learning	• Family as community • Importance of ethnic and religious traditions • Memory as community builder	• Envisioning a caring classroom community • Good & poor listening • Respecting other people's opinions • Using put-ups; avoiding put-downs • Observation

The Keeping Quilt, by Patricia Polacco.
Simon and Schuster, 1988.

SUMMARY

The narrator tells of her Great-Grandma Anna, who as a child came to America from "backhome Russia." Anna is confused by the New World, but determined to make it her home. As she adapts to life in the United States, soon all she has left of backhome Russia are her dress and her babushka. When she outgrows the dress, her mother says that they will make a quilt from the dress, babushka, and the old clothes of other relatives. The quilt will "help us always remember home." The neighborhood women gather for a quilting bee. We follow the life of the quilt as it is used as a tablecloth on the Sabbath, later as a picnic blanket the day that Great-Grandpa Sasha proposes to Anna, as a huppa (wedding canopy) at Anna's wedding, as a receiving blanket for Anna's new daughter. The quilt serves the same functions for two more generations of women, as the family moves from the Eastern seaboard to the Midwest, taking the customs of backhome Russia and Orthodox Judaism and adapting to new cultures and communities. Anna dies at age 98, and the narrator's mother, Mary Ellen, inherits the quilt, taking it with her as she leaves home. When Mary Ellen marries, the quilt is again the huppa. The quilt welcomes the narrator, Patricia, into the world, and serves as the tablecloth for her first birthday party, for her imaginary play as a child, and finally for her huppa. The quilt welcomes her own daughter to the world and there is the promise that the daughter will leave home and take it with her. Throughout the book there is also the symbolic presence of bread, salt, and a gold coin at each wedding, representing a hope that the couple will not know hunger, that their lives will have flavor, and that they will not know poverty.

COMMENT

This book is a moving tale of traditions and communities confronting a new culture and modernity. The first family emigrates and makes the transition from a rural community to an urban one. They must adjust to the faster pace of life. Still, their neighbors "were just like them." That is, they were Orthodox Jews from Russia. We see the tight-knit community in action as the women gather to sew the quilt. We read that Anna learns to speak English, but her parents don't. She is their key to the New World, as she must translate for them. We see the rituals that keep the family together, the prayers over the Sabbath dinner, the challah and chicken soup, the engagement ritual, as Sasha offers her symbols of their future life (a gold coin, a dried flower, and a piece of rock salt wrapped in a handkerchief), the wedding at which men and women celebrate separately. Anna's life is not much different from her mother's, and she brings up her daughter to "keep the Sabbath and to cook and clean and do washing," in preparation for marriage. But when Anna's daughter, Carle, marries, the men and women celebrate together at her wedding, although they still don't dance together. Carle and George move to a farm in Michigan, bringing the family back to its rural roots but in a very different environment. The religion sustains the family as Great-Grandma Anna dies. Carle's daughter, Mary Ellen, leaves home. She is not leaving to get married, and we sense that she is a modern woman making her way in the world. At her marriage, "for the first time, friends who were not Jews came to the wedding." Still, Mary Ellen carries the gold, bread, and salt in her bouquet. Mary Ellen's daughter, Patricia, wants to hear the stories of the people whose clothes make up the quilt.

She feels connected to her Russian roots despite her upbringing in the suburbs. At her wedding, men and women dance together, and the faces in the crowd are more diverse than at the earlier weddings. We can guess from her husband's name, and we know from other books by the same author, that she married a man of Italian heritage, so we know that she is also moving out from the people of her ancestors.

Throughout the book, we see women as caretakers of the traditions. For instance, Patricia clearly has an older brother, but it is she who will inherit the quilt. We can look at ways that men and women carry on the traditions of their respective communities. We see the support that the close-knit immigrant communities give, and we see the younger people move into the New World and forge new communities. We know from other books by this author that she grew up in a multiracial neighborhood and lives a life quite different from that of her great-grandmother.

 Because all of us in the United States come from immigrants—either willing or unwilling—and many in the classroom may be recent immigrants themselves, this book offers a wonderful opportunity to explore the communities we come from, our own family, ethnic, and religious rituals and traditions as well as the process by which we build new communities and forge new rituals. We can look at these processes in our classroom and among our friends and families.

Book Talk

READ ALOUD

Previewing the book

Look at the cover of the book. Ask the students to tell you everything they notice about the drawing. What do they think this book will be about? Where will the story take place? Who are the main characters? What is the quilt keeping? Look at the first drawing on the inside. What do we think the story is about now? Ask the children to write down what they notice about the picture. Read the description of the author. Has anyone read other books of hers?   Make a list of the books on the board. We know that this author writes about her life and the lives of people she has known or to whom she is related. Given the description of the author's background, can we guess where the people in the picture come from?

Reading and responding to the book[3]

Read the book slowly, giving the students time to look at the pictures. Stop occasionally and ask the students what's happening. Stop at key points and ask them what they think will happen next, or what they notice about the pictures.

After you have finished the story, ask the students to pair up with their read-aloud partner and talk about the book. What interests them? What do they want to know more about?

Deepening students' understanding of the book

Ask the students to recall what happened in the book. They may have questions that the book doesn't answer, (for example, about religious traditions). What do they think the book is mainly about? They may say that it is about a quilt, which is certainly true. However, we are looking at the quilt as a symbol of the community that anchors people as they move out into the world. It can represent the traditions and history of Patricia's family. Explain that in the second reading[4] you want them to focus on what the pictures tell us about the traditions and the people as well as what the words tell us. Ask them to think about how the characters are feeling as they start new lives or learn the stories of their ancestors.

---

[3] There are different approaches to read-alouds. You may wish to read the book through without stopping at all. You may read through, pausing only when the students ask a question or look puzzled. Or you may choose to do an interactive read-aloud in which you pause from time to time in the reading to point out something, to ask what is happening or what the students think will happen next or what choices the characters could make. Choose the option you prefer. Except in a few cases, the suggestions that follow are based on the assumption that you are reading the book through without pauses except for students' questions. If you decide to do an interactive read-aloud, you can refer to the suggestions in *Deepening students' understanding of the book* for possible stopping places.

[4] Before you do the second reading of the book (or, if you are doing only one reading), you may want to choose a question or two for the students to follow and to answer informally in writing before discussion. Or you might ask them to jot down a few thoughts on a question you ask after the reading. This informal writing often encourages more students to speak during the discussion and allows all students to voice their thoughts, not just those who are comfortable speaking in groups.

The quilt is the major symbol in the book, but we see other symbols also, particularly on p. 11, when Sasha proposes to Anna and again on p. 14 when Carle receives gold, flower, salt, and bread. There are also other rituals besides marriage, such as on p. 10, when the family celebrates the Sabbath or when Great-Grandma Anna dies and the family says prayers for the dead (p. 21).

We see a lot of changes in the pictures, as clothing styles change along with traditions (p. 16, men and women are celebrating together, as opposed to earlier, on p. 12, when the attendees were in separate sections).

Patricia makes up stories about the animals in the quilt—possibly one of her early forays into fiction—and her mother tells her stories about the people whose clothing makes up the quilt. How has Patricia's mother learned the stories? How do we find out the stories of our families and communities?

After you finish the second reading, give the students a chance to share any additional observations and thoughts. How have they felt about traditions in their family? What does it feel like when traditions change or the family doesn't do the things it used to do?

Connecting the book to students' lives[5]

Discussion: Most communities have rituals for marking major life events. What rituals have the students been part of or witnessed or heard about? Make a list. For example, a baptism, a bris, First Communion, graduations, Scouting ceremonies, becoming a citizen of the United States, Sweet Sixteen parties, Quinceañero, a bar or bat mitzvah, weddings, funerals, swearing in of the President of the United States.

What are "rituals" or "traditions" that we have in our classroom? These might be special ways of doing things that we practice (for example, how we recognize a birthday, how we acknowledge another's work or contribution to the group, what we do when we gather for circle time). If someone new were to join the class, what would you tell them about our classroom rituals or traditions. Are there rituals or traditions that you would like the class to have?

Are there any symbols in our classroom – objects that carry a special meaning? (For, example, a chime that invites the class to come to silence? A saying that reminds us what to do next? An object that we look at when we need to "cool down"?) If you were to create a symbol that had a special meaning for the class, what would it be?

Does anyone in the class have a quilt in the family? Has anyone ever made a quilt? The first quilts were probably made because people were poor and had to use all the scraps of material that they had. They would save rags and then piece them together. There is even a type of quilt called a "crazy quilt" that has no particular design and is just bits of cloth sewn

---

[5] Most of the ideas in this section in all the units are suited to drawing and writing activities. Young children may draw and then dictate or write a caption or story. At all ages, the writing may be informal, as in a reading-response journal or just a regular paper or notebook or, if a seed idea seems appropriate, students may work more on a piece. Writing is a powerful way for each student to think about ideas, and we encourage its use.

together. Other quilts have designs and color schemes. Ask students to pair up and describe a quilt they could make about their family. What pieces of clothing would they use from their family members? Are there adults who could bring in quilts and tell stories about them to the class?

Why did the girls in Patricia's family get the quilt? Are there traditions about what girls usually inherit vs. what boys inherit? Why do the students think this is so?

What other books has this author written that talk about tradition? Some students can do an author study and report back to the class.

Writing: Ask students to pick one ritual they have seen or been part of and write about it. What were some of the symbols used in the ritual?

Do students have items that have been passed down in their families? Ask them to interview their parents or guardians and get a story. It may be an item that the family no longer has but that once belonged to them and about which there is a story. Ask them to find out about family traditions. Have them write about the objects and/or the traditions and make a book to share with the class. Do any of these items or traditions symbolize anything?

Make a class paper quilt with photographs or drawings. Each student makes a block of the quilt. Ask each student to make a border of words that describe her or him. When the quilt is finished, ask students to look for the differences and similarities among themselves.

Suggest that they write a letter to the quilt. What would they say to it? What do they want to ask it?

ROLE-PLAY

The students will work in pairs. One will play the role of Patricia as an adult; the other, her child at age ten. (Boys can play the roles of parent who explains and child who listens, too.) Patricia has the quilt and is explaining it to her child for the first time. The child listens well, asks questions, is interested in learning about his or her ancestors and family traditions. After the students have worked in pairs, ask for volunteers to present their role-plays to the group.

Applied Learning

SOCIAL AND EMOTIONAL LEARNING

Lesson 1

Objectives

Students will
- practice paying close attention to others and their classroom environment;
- define "community" as it applies to what we are trying to create in the classroom;
- identify the qualities of an ideal classroom community and make a quilt to express their vision

Materials
- Agenda on chart paper or the chalkboard
- Hugg-A-Planet
- Chart paper for recording students' ideas about how building community is like making a quilt
- Drawing paper and markers for designing patches of a quilt

Gathering: Name Game

Have the students stand in a circle. Toss a Hugg-A-Planet or other soft object to a student. The student who catches it calls out her or his full name and then everyone yells, "Yes!" The student then throws the object to someone else until all have had a chance to say their names. Encourage students to pay close attention to who has the Hugg-A-Planet. How do you know when that person is ready to throw it? What can that person look for to know if someone else is ready to receive it?

Check agenda

Go over the objectives and the agenda.

Deepening our understanding of community

Review with the students the steps involved in making a quilt. Then ask for their first thoughts to complete this sentence: Building community in the classroom is like making a quilt because ________________. Elicit at least ten quick ideas. Then discuss: What's your vision of the kind of community we'd like to have in our classroom? What insights might we take from *The Keeping Quilt* about how to create the kind of community we want?

One insight that this book contributes to our understanding of community is that we are not only a part of what is happening now, but of what has happened and will happen. Our classroom has traditions that have come from previous classes. We will pass on and create traditions for classes to come. Ask the students to write about a person who is a part of one of their communities who is no longer living or physically present in our lives. What did that person give to their community? These could be people from whom we learned something, who gave us something of themselves, who inspired or encouraged us in some way.

Making a classroom quilt: envisioning a caring community

Ask the students to take a few moments in silence and picture in their mind's eye images that one would see in a caring classroom community: What specific things would students be doing? How would they be relating to each other? Ask them to draw or write about their images in their reading response journals, and then share them with a partner.

Have each student design a patch for a quilt expressing their image. They are to draw it first, then make it in fabric, or if that's not an option, they can complete it as a drawing or collage. Once the patches are done, sew them into a quilt or arrange them into a quilt on the wall or bulletin board over the title, "Classroom Community, Our Vision."

Evaluation

What was the most fun about today's lesson? Ask for a couple of volunteers to share their thoughts with the group.

Closing: High five

High five: You and the students stand in a circle. Give the student to your right a "high five." That student gives a high five to the next student, and so it goes, all around the circle.

Lesson 2

Objectives

Students will
- identify behaviors that make for poor listening
- identify behaviors that make for good listening
- develop a chart of guidelines for good listening
- express their opinions and see that differences of opinion are okay

Materials

- Agenda on chart paper or the chalkboard
- Two or three soft balls for the "Group Juggle"
- Chart paper for writing "Guidelines for Good Listening"
- Signs for the "Think Differently" exercise ("Strongly Agree," "Strongly Disagree," "Not sure")

Gathering: Group juggle

The students stand in a circle. Throw the ball to a student and ask that student to throw it to someone who hasn't had it yet. Stop the action. Tell the students to remember who threw the ball to them and to whom they threw the ball. Start the action again, with the student who has the ball throwing it to someone else and so on until all the students have had the ball and the last one has thrown it back to you. Now start the ball again, throwing it to the same student as before, who throws it to the same person s/he threw it to, and so on, following the same pattern as before. Practice moving the ball around the circle until the group can do it fast and well. Then, start the ball going again, and after it has reached the third or fourth person, start a second ball going in the same pattern. If you want to make things really interesting, start a third or even a fourth ball.

After a few rounds with more than one ball, collect the balls. Ask the class what it took to make the Group Juggle work successfully. This may lead to comments about the need to focus and pay attention. How do noticing and paying attention to others help build community?

Check agenda

Go over the objectives and the agenda.

Good and poor listening

One of the cornerstones of community is being able to listen to each other. When Anna came to the United States she couldn't speak the language. She had to listen extra hard to be able to understand, and people had to listen hard to her in order to understand her.

Ask for a volunteer from the class to come up front and tell you something. While the person is talking, model poor listening (looking away, fidgeting with clothes or hair, doing something else). Ask how the person felt while you were doing this. Ask the class what the class saw. Now have the person tell you the same information, but model good listening, (attention focused on speaker, positive body language, no interrupting). Make a good-listening checklist to post on the wall.

Think differently

People in the United States take pride in having many different traditions and communities. However, we know that not everyone shares the same needs, traditions, and opinions. Ask, what is an opinion? It's a strong belief that people have, sometimes based on fact and sometimes not.

Designate one corner of the room for "strongly agree," the opposite corner for "strongly disagree," and the middle for "not sure." Make signs if necessary. Ask the students to think for a few moments in silence about their opinion on the statement. Then they will go to the appropriate place according to whether they agree with the statement, disagree, or aren't sure. Try to think of statements on which student will have a range of opinions. Once the students have taken their places, ask for volunteers from each location to explain their opinion. Encourage some dialogue among students with differing opinions. If students change their minds in the course of the discussion, they can change places. Here are some suggested statements:

- Children shouldn't be required to do homework
- Children shouldn't be required to attend school
- Children should be limited to one hour of screen time a day
- Children should wear uniforms in school
- Children should be allowed to chew gum and eat candy in class

Evaluation

What's one thing you'll do differently as a result of today's lesson? Ask for several volunteers to share their thoughts with the group.

Closing: Pass the sound*

Begin by making a sound. "Pass" the sound to a student. Ask the student to imitate the sound your are making and then change it into another sound. S/he passes it to another person who repeats the new sound and changes it again. Continue around the group, encouraging each person to listen closely and observe how the person before them is making the sound.

* From *The Friendly Classroom for a Small Planet* by Priscilla Prutzman, et al. New Society Publishers, Gabriola Island, BC, Canada. Copyright © 1988 Children's Creative Response to Conflict, PO Box 271, Nyack, NY 10960. T: (845) 353-1796 / F: (845) 358-4924. Used by permission.

Lesson 3

Objectives

Students will
- define "put-up" and "put-down"
- identify the feelings that put-downs and put-ups tend to set off, and the physical signs of those feelings;
- identify people in their lives whom they appreciate

Materials Needed

- Agenda on chart paper or the chalkboard
- Two hearts made from construction paper (see pattern at the end of the unit) and tape to fasten them to your chest
- Markers of various colors

Gathering: New and Good

What's something good that you've experienced lately? This could be a small thing like enjoying the blue sky on a beautiful day or seeing a flower on the way to school or something major like getting your black belt in karate.

Give the students a minute or two to talk with a partner, then ask for several volunteers to tell their "new and good" to the group.

Check agenda

Go over the objectives and the agenda.

Put-ups and put-downs

If the students don't already know about put-downs, introduce the idea that a put-down is a negative comment about a person. Elicit examples of put-downs (but don't write them down so as not to reinforce them). Ask the children what they think a put-up is. Elicit examples of put-ups. Make a chart of put-ups. Explain that in our classroom, put-downs are not allowed. Put-ups are welcome. When you and the students hear people using put-ups, you can acknowledge them and add them to the chart.

Point out that we often hear put-downs in everyday life and in the media. Ask students to collect put-downs and put-ups for the next two days. Hand out slips of paper and ask them to write the put-down or put-up on the paper. Use different colored paper. At the end of the two days, ask everyone to put all the papers in two same-size glass jars. See how many are in each jar. Read some from each jar and ask how the person who heard it must have felt.

Have a Heart

Make two hearts from construction paper. Explain that our feelings and our classroom community are greatly affected by how we talk to each other. This exercise illustrates the effects of put-downs.

Tape one of the hearts to your chest. Tell the students a story like the one below, tailored to their age and experience. Each time the child in the story experiences a put-down, rip off a piece of the heart and let it fall to the floor. By the end of the story, the heart will be in pieces. Discuss: What is the heart a symbol for? How is _____________ feeling? If you could see _____________ right now, what do you think she might look like? Encourage discussion of facial expression, posture, how she might be moving, and other clues that might help you know what she is feeling. (Students can pantomime what they think her face and posture might look like.) Have you ever had a day like this?

Now tape the second heart to your chest and retell the story with the students supplying put-ups instead of put-downs. When the child receives put-ups, color in the heart with crayons or markers of various colors. Discuss: How is _____________ feeling now? Again, ask what would be the clues – facial expression, posture, movements – that would let you know how she feels? Have students pantomime these. What does this exercise suggest for our classroom?

Story for the Have a Heart exercise

Jane* had not slept well, and when her father called, she didn't get up. A few minutes later, her father shouted, "Get up, lazybones!" When Jane went into the kitchen for breakfast, her brother was just pouring the last of the cereal into his bowl. "That's what you get for oversleeping," he teased. Jane dressed in a new combination she thought looked cool, but when her sister saw her, she laughed. "That looks stupid," she said. Jane changed clothes, grabbed her book bag, and ran out the door to school. She decided to take a short cut. "Hey, what are you doing around this block?" some boy called to her. "We don't like your type around here." "You're late!" the teacher said when she came into her classroom. He wrote her name on the board. Later, the teacher asked her to read aloud. When she said one of the words wrong, some of the kids laughed. At lunch, when she went to sit down with some girls, they said, "No room here. You'll have to sit over there." On the way home from school, Jane was running along and tripped over a crack in the pavement. She want sprawling down on the street and ripped a hole in her pants. When her mother saw Jane, she saw the hole before she saw the rest of her. "You ruined your pants," she said. "I can't keep you in decent clothes!"

* Substitute a name for Jane that is not the name of anyone in your class.

Evaluation

What's one thing you'll do differently as a result of the lesson today?

Closing: Someone I appreciate

Each of us has people in our lives whom we appreciate. Who is one of those people for you? Give the students a minute or two to talk in pairs and then ask several volunteers to tell the group.

Additional Activities

Symbols

Remind the class of the way that bread was used in weddings in *The Keeping Quilt* to symbolize the hope that the couple would never know hunger. Have the class create visual symbols that can serve as reminders for them. For example, they might think of symbols to remind them to use put ups or to listen with full attention.

Hillel the Wise

Tell or read or have the children read the story *Hillel the Wise* (see handout at the end of the unit) and explain that people all over the world in various countries and cultures share a similar belief. How does this rule apply to the people in *The Keeping Quilt* and how might it apply in our classroom? There are many places in the world where it is the custom to give the best of everything to the guests even if they are strangers. Being respectful of each other and each other's talents is a key theme. We respect what each person brings to our community. Would this be a good rule for our classroom? Why? Why not?

Other books about quilts

Have students read other books about quilts. Some students can do a genre study and report back to the class. What do quilts seem to symbolize in these stories? In the past few decades there have been groups of people who have made quilts to symbolize their hopes and to honor their members. The AIDS quilt, made up of hundreds of pieces created by people from around the country, is so large that it takes up space larger than a football field. The National Peace Quilt, made by children in all fifty states, was given to elected leaders to help them think more about ways to create a peaceful world.

Seeing quilts in a museum

Patricia Polacco's quilt is a memory quilt. Many quilts also tell stories. Modern quilts are often very abstract and multimedia. Quilts exist in some form in every culture. Plan a trip to a craft museum to look at quilts.

Writing about experiences with people like us & different from us

Anna lived with people who were just like her family. Patricia lived in a community where people were different. Have you ever had the experience of being with people who were all like you? Write about the good things you like about that. (Examples can include same-sex events, being with a religious, cultural, or ethnic group, being with a same-age group.) Write about an experience of being with a group that was different from you but where you had a good time.

Consider having your students keep a 4Rs journal

Writing (drawing for younger students) is an excellent way to reinforce and consolidate learning. A journal enables students to put all of their Book Talk writing in one place. You can also give them a few minutes after each 4Rs lesson to jot down a few thoughts about what they're taking away or how they're planning to use what they've just learned. If a student tries a new skill, s/he might want to write about what happened. Did it bring a positive result? If a student is stuck in a conflict with someone, s/he might want to do some writing to sort it out and imagine some solutions. You can give them standard journals and encourage them to decorate them.

By having students keep journals, you will be introducing them to a habit or practice that can serve them well the rest of their lives.

Related Books

Patricia Polacco has written many books that deal with community. She is an excellent person for an author study.

There are many, many quilt-themed books. Here are the titles of a few:

The Boy and the Quilt by Shirley Kurtz, illustrated by Cheryl Benner

The Canada Geese Quilt by Natalie Kinsey-Warnock, illustrated by Leslie Bowman

Dancing at the Louvre by Faith Ringgold (10th anniversary edition has five more pages)

Firetalking (Meet the Author) by Patricia Polacco

Fly Away Home by Eve Bunting, illustrated by Ron Himler

The Josefina Story Quilt by Eleanor Coerr, illustrated by Bruce Degen

The Log Cabin Quilt by Ellen Howard, illustrated by Ronald Himler

A Name on the Quilt: A Story of Remembrance by Jeannine Atkins, Tad Hills, illustrator

The Names Project: the AIDS Quilt by Larry Dane Brimner

The Patchwork Quilt by Valerie Flournoy, illustrated by Jerry Pinkney

The Quilt Story by Tony Johnston, illustrated by Tomie De Paola

Pattern for
Have a Heart

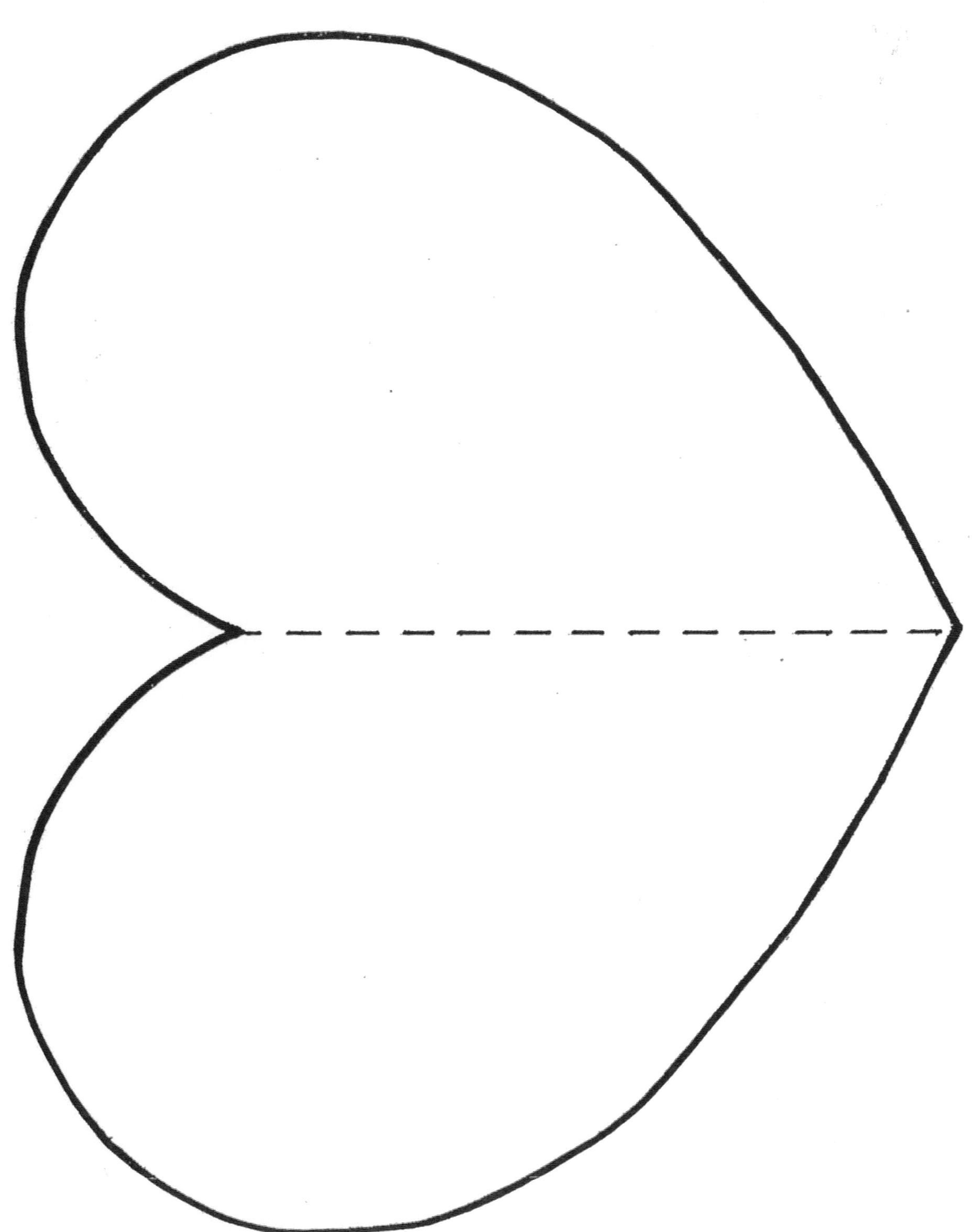

Hillel the Wise

There once was a very wise and learned teacher named Hillel. Now, Rabbi Hillel was not only a wise teacher, he was a good and patient teacher. His reputation had spread as far as King Herod's palace. There was a young man in Herod's palace who did not like to study, who did not want to learn. But he did like to make fun of others, and he did like to gamble. So one day he made a bet with his friends that he could show that Rabbi Hillel was not as wise and patient as he was supposed to be. He wagered 400 zuzim that he could make Hillel angry. For three days he asked Hillel annoying questions, and each time, the rabbi answered patiently and with great wisdom. The young man was afraid he would lose the bet and have to pay 400 zuzim. He stayed up all night thinking of a way to make Hillel angry. The next day, he burst into the study house and stood in front of Hillel. He hopped up and down, saying, "Rabbi, Rabbi, can you teach me the whole of Torah while I stand on one foot?" All the other students were amazed. They spent years studying Torah, the holy book. Hillel stayed calm. He looked at the young man and said, "That which is hateful unto you, do not do it to your neighbor. That is the whole of Torah. The rest is commentary. Now go and learn."

Many religious traditions have a similar teaching. Christianity uses a "golden rule" similar to Rabbi Hillel's: "Do unto others as you would have them do unto you." Muslims have a teaching in the holy book the Koran that says, "Repel the evil with what is better, and you will see that the worst of enemies can become the best of friends."

Adapted from *While Standing on One Foot, Puzzle Stories and Wisdom Tales from the Jewish Tradition*, by Nina Jaffe and Steve Zeitlin. Henry Holt and Company, Inc., 1993.

5

Unit 2 Theme

Understanding & Managing Feelings

Unit 2 Book Selection

Mysterious Traveler by Mal Peet and Elspeth Graham
Candlewick Press, 2013

Activities

- Feelings Web and Feelings Charades
- Stories about feelings
- Feelings Barometer
- Anger Triggers
- Squeeze Relax
- Responses to Anger
- Anger Choices ◆ Anger Stories ◆ Anger Signals
- Brainstorming Ways to Cool Down
  - ✓ Self-talk
  - ✓ Abdominal Breathing
  - ✓ Drawing and Gallery Walk
  - ✓ Plan 1-2-3
- Additional Activities

Introduction

We all have feelings; like conflict, feelings are part of life. But feelings don't need to control our lives or dictate our actions. When feelings come up, we can choose whether or not to act on them and, if so, how. This is one of the most important principles in creating community and in dealing well with conflict.

Understanding that they have feelings and naming them is not always easy for children. Often adults will tell a child, "Be quiet, that didn't hurt," or "That's not something to be upset about," or "Of course you love your baby brother," when the child is feeling something completely different. Children need to acknowledge their feelings and learn to handle them. They need to know that others also have feelings that are expressed in tone of voice, facial expression, and body language. They need to be able to think ahead to the consequences of acting on feelings, to be able to try to predict whether a proposed action will have the intended result.

Much of our energy in the classroom and life in general goes toward negative feelings. We need to celebrate positive feelings and their impact on the community.

Literature offers many opportunities to talk about feelings, as we analyze the actions of characters and the feelings evoked in us, the readers.

In any discussion of conflict and of feelings, anger always comes up and therefore deserves special attention. The American Heritage Dictionary defines anger as a feeling of extreme displeasure, hostility, indignation, or exasperation toward someone or something. Behind anger may lie feelings of fear and hurt. Everyone has anger triggers, but the triggers are different for different people. It is particularly useful for us to become aware of what triggers our anger and that of others so that we can manage the anger rather than letting it control us. Anger is useful in letting us know that needs are not being met. But when anger goes up, thinking tends to go down. We can learn strategies for cooling down so that we can express our anger in a constructive way that respects the other person and is most likely to lead to a positive result.

Strategies for reducing anger include recognizing that you're angry (by recognizing the anger cues); centering (taking deep breaths, counting to ten); focusing attention on something pleasant (thinking pleasant thoughts, visualizing a favorite place, etc.); and talking to yourself in positive ways ("I can handle this" or "We can work it out").

How to Calm Down When You're Angry

- Leave the situation for a while, saying that you'll be back when you can think more clearly

- Count to ten

- Take deep breaths, focusing your eyes on something pleasant near you

- Talk to yourself: "I can handle this," "I'm not going to let this person make me do something stupid."

Once we have calmed down, we can decide what action, if any, to take. It's possible that the situation really just requires a calming-down period. If, however, the situation requires action, that action can be taken in an assertive, not aggressive, way, so that it does not escalate the situation.

Anger can be used constructively to change situations. We need to hold fast to and channel what could be called "righteous anger," the indignation at actions and conditions in the world that are unfair. It is this anger that has fueled the work of many well-known religious leaders, visionaries, and social activists.

In this unit

	Ideas	Skills
Literacy	• Quest theme • Metaphors and similes • Dialogue • Place as a character	• Dialogue • Point of view • Use of simile and metaphor
Social and Emotional Learning	• All human beings experience a wide range of feelings. • Identifying and naming our feelings gives us more control over them. • When feelings arise, we have choices about how to respond. • When we experience strong feelings, we don't always think clearly. • We can learn ways to cool down so that we can think more clearly about the smartest thing to do.	• Observation • Naming feelings • Reading feelings • Noticing physical sensations that accompany feelings • Identifying our anger triggers • Strategies for cooling down so that we can think more clearly • Self-talk • Abdominal breathing • Plan 1-2-3

Mysterious Traveler, by Mal Peet and Elspeth Graham. Illus. by P.J. Lynch. Candlewick Press; text copyright © 2013 by Mal Peet and Elspeth Graham; illustrations copyright © 2013 by P.J. Lynch.

SUMMARY

We are plunged into a mystery with the first page. Five travelers ride across the desert, but there are six camels. The riderless camel carries a treasure. What it is, we do not know, but the men who guard it are scared and riding fast. Suddenly, a sandstorm engulfs them, and they disappear. The desert holds its secret.

On the edge of the desert, Issa, a renowned guide, greets the sunrise with the awe he feels every day at the beauty of the desert and the possibilities of life. Today, though, he senses something different. There has been a storm. His eye catches sight of a fragment of richly embroidered ribbon not of the region. He determines to go in search of the owner. He finds the riderless camel, Jin-Jin, still guarding the treasure, which turns out to be a baby girl with "huge black pearls for eyes." Around her neck the baby wears half of a gold pendant with strange writing on it. Looking up at the sky, Issa asks, "Why did you send such a gift to an old man?"

The answer is not obvious, for, although it is not stated explicitly, in Issa's community, a girl will never be able to succeed him as a guide as a son would have. Nevertheless, Issa and the baby, whom he names Mariama, grow to love each other. The townspeople decide that she is his granddaughter, and he does not deny it. He tells those who ask why he brings a girl along on his work that she is "a child of the desert." Years pass, and she learns "everything that Issa knew." They are a team.

But Issa is growing old, and his sight fails him. Now he knows why the gift was given: at first he had questioned God's plan, thinking "it was unfair for an old man to be burdened with a child." Then, "I thought the gift was love," he says, but now, he realizes that he can understand it only afterward, "in darkness." "Yes, Baba," Mariama says, "I was sent to be your eyes."

Now the two are inseparable. She must hone her language to tell Issa exactly where the landmarks are, and he, with his memory, can still guide travelers. They retain their livelihood. But worry gnaws at Issa. One day he will die, and who will marry a poor orphan girl?

The answer to his unvoiced prayer seems to come in the form of three travelers who offer a bag of pearls in exchange for passage through a dangerous valley. They are in a hurry and refuse to take the safe path with the trading caravan. When they realize that Issa is blind, they grab back the pearls and storm out, believing that the villagers made fools of them by sending them to Issa. The youngest of the three, Abbas, who is clearly the leader, has a "magic stone" that points northward. They put their faith in it. "Birds have the same magic stone in their heads," observes Issa, but they can "fly over mountains," while humans cannot. He knows they will soon be lost, and his sense of the wind is that a storm is approaching.

Even though the travelers have insulted him, he insists on going after them. Sure enough, the storm comes upon them, as it did upon the travelers at the beginning of the story. Issa directs Mariama and the strangers to the cleft in the mountain where he first found her. The strangers are grateful, but he merely advises them to go with the caravan as soon as they have rested.

Two days later, the young man comes to offer the pearls to Issa for saving their lives. Issa refuses the reward. The young man lays the bag at Mariama's feet, motioning to her to keep it, then, startled, aggressively asks where she got her pendant. She clutches it, not sure what to say, for until now, only she and Issa have known of it. Issa, hearing the urgency in the young man's voice, realizes that he may know the story of Mariama's origin and decides to tell him the story of finding her. Ecstatic, the young man responds that he has been searching for his long-lost sister, a princess from a neighboring kingdom. She had been presumed dead, but their father had never given up hope. He pulls out the other half of the locket from around his neck and announces as if it is a fait accompli *that he will take her back to the palace. Mariama's "smile clouded over." "Grandfather needs me. I can't leave him here alone." Issa insists that he will manage, but Abbas understands the bonds of love and says they must all return together. The story ends as Issa learns the new landscape of the palace and enjoys "seeing these things through the eyes of Mariama, on whose young shoulder his old hand rests."*

COMMENT

We are in the realm of the fairy tale, the story of the lost princess, reimagined by the authors. We can look at how the authors created a modern fairy tale using conventions of traditional folklore in which a prince finds a long-lost maiden (Snow White, Sleeping Beauty). In this more modern version, though, the prince's quest purpose is not to marry her but to bring her back to her birth family.

We can note the evocative names (Issa is the name *Jesús* in Arabic; Mariama is a West African name that means "gift of God"; and Abbas can be interpreted as "lion" or "king"; Jin-Jin could even be a play on the word Jinn/genie or protective spirit). We are in Timbuktu (although it is never named), a synonym in the Western mind for adventure, mystery, and a meeting of many worlds. We can talk about the emotions that each character experiences as the story unfolds. We can look at point of view, starting with that of the camel in the beginning and moving to that of Issa, shifting occasionally to Mariama as she observes the strangers.

We can examine the moral choices made by each character (Jin-Jin's willingness to sacrifice for Mariama; Issa's willingness to help the strangers even though they have shamed him; Mariama's devotion to her adopted grandfather; Abbas's persistence in fulfilling his father's command).

We can learn about simile (pearls "like an angel's tears," silence "as thick as fleece," making the camel run "like the wind") and metaphor (the womb of the cave, the various references to eyes and seeing, talk of riches and gifts).

We can talk about use of place as a major character, i.e., the desert. Would this story have been as compelling if it had taken place in a jungle or a busy urban setting? We can talk about foreshadowing, about story twists, about what makes for a satisfying ending. We can note that in fairy tales there is almost always a happy ending for the heroes, whereas in other literature there is usually some ambiguity about the happiness.

In Unit 3 of this curriculum, on listening, the protagonist cannot understand the language of those who have landed in his country but must "listen" to their actions and body language. When we reach that unit, we can refer back to Issa and the way he "sees" the desert both while he can actually see it and when he has to "see" it through Mariama's words.

Book Talk

READ-ALOUD

Previewing the book

Show the cover of the book. Because these authors are British, it is unlikely that students will be familiar with their work. Read the jacket notes about the author and illustrator and show the dedication page and title page. What clues are there in the pictures (students may not realize that the pouch contains treasure)? Do we think that this story will take place in our country or another country? Do we have any clues about the time period? If there is a map of the world, show Timbuktu on the map and show how traders would come from throughout the known world to exchange goods. The city's Golden Age was in the fifteenth and sixteenth centuries, which gives us some idea of when the story might be set.

Introduce the students to words that may be unfamiliar, for example:
- caravans
- oasis
- Qur'an
- pendant
- minaret
- sandstorm

Reading and responding to the book

Read the book slowly and allow time to look at the pictures, absorb the moods, and notice the details.

At various points in the story, pause also to ask students what they think will happen next.

After you have finished reading the story, ask the students, What would you like to say about this story? Do you have any questions?

Deepening the students' understanding of the book

Ask the students to recall the main events of the story. What themes do they see? Encourage as many ideas and interpretations as you can. There are many ways to look at this work. It is a modern story with a modern sensibility written in a mythic style. On one level, it is a good adventure. On others, it is a quest book as well as a coming-of-age story. What's different in this case is that Abbas is on the quest and Mariama is the one who comes of age. Quest heroes usually carry some talisman or weapon (in this case, the pendant and the compass) and often find that what they want is right under their eyes (Abbas has to fail first because of his pride before he "finds" Mariama, toward whom he was drawn: "There was a question in his face, but he did not ask it.") Mariama must choose between riches and loyalty. Both stories are reflected through the thoughts and actions of Issa.

For this unit, we want to look at the emotions the characters must grapple with, most significantly, Issa, who experiences fear, despair, loneliness, and anger along with love, awe, and joy. We want to talk about Issa's and others' strategies for dealing with their feelings.

Tell the students that you will read the story again, now paying special attention to the emotions they believe the different characters could be feeling. Stop at appropriate points and ask for ideas about the emotions (start in the opening scene with Jin-Jin's fear and sense of responsibility; the baby Mariama, who may be feeling safe with Jin-Jin or may be terrified; and Issa, who has lived alone and never imagined finding a baby in a cave).

Because the characters of Issa and Mariama are paragons of virtue, the more negative aspects of anger and contempt are shown by the travelers. Probe for the travelers' feelings of disappointment beneath the anger or entitlement that they show.

Here are some places where you might pause during the second reading and ask students how they think the characters might be feeling:

- the opening scene in which the riders are being chased and then realize they face an even greater danger: a desert storm
- when Mariama realizes that Issa is going blind: "Her blood turned as cold as water from the well."
- when the man with hawklike nose expresses disbelief that Issa is blind: "Mariama felt hot blood rise to her face."
- when the man with the scarred face says, "Pah!" and tears the pouch of pearls from Issa's hand
- when the storm is approaching and Mariama is looking for the cave where they will hide but doesn't see it at first: "Mariama swallowed her fear."
- when the young traveler (Abbas) sees Mariama's pendant and asks where she got it: "Mariama was alarmed."
- when Mariama fears that she will be separated from Issa: "Mariama sat folded in a kind of terror"
- when Abbas puts his pendant next to Mariama's and they fit together: "Understanding filled her, like a sunrise."

Connecting the book to students' lives

Discussion: When Mariama can't find the entrance to the cave where they can get protection from the sandstorm, she "swallowed her fear" and kept on looking and finally found the entrance just in time. Ask the students, "What does it mean to swallow your fear?" Ask the students to share with their read-aloud partners a time when they were afraid of something. What were they afraid of? What did they do? How did it turn out?

When each person finishes speaking, suggest that they ask their partner to take a deep breath in unison with them. Deep breathing can be a way to calm and center oneself after talking about an emotional topic. It also allows the listener a few moments to fully take in the speaker's story, and may encourage empathic listening. (It may be helpful to model this by telling the class a story about a time you were afraid, and inviting the whole group to take a deep breath with you at the end.)

Writing: Ask students to write a story about the time they were afraid. Their story should include where they were, what they were afraid of, what they did, what help they got from others (if any), and how it turned out.

There are a number of places in the book where natural phenomena are described in rich detail. For example, the sunrise Issa witnesses is described in this way: "At first it was a tiny red glimpse, as if someone had lit a fire among the distant hills. Slowly at first, then more quickly, it grew and swelled until it floated above the hills like a fat, shivery bubble. The colors of the desert came alive…" In describing the scene in this way, the author is using what is sometimes called "mindful" seeing. Being mindful involves being fully aware of yourself and your surroundings in each moment and being completely present to what you are experiencing. Draw students' attention to this passage and have them write a rich description of some phenomenon – perhaps a sunrise, sunset, a thunderstorm, a strong wind. They might describe the phenomenon in terms of what it looks like, sounds like, smells like, etc.

ROLE-PLAY

Divide the class into groups of four and have each group pick a scene that it will practice and then present to the class.

Applied Learning

Lesson 1

Objectives

Students will
- recall words that name feelings experienced by characters in the story
- share other "feelings words" they know to create a "feelings web"
- practice expressing feelings and reading feelings
- recognize that there are sometimes connections between feelings and physical sensations.
- tell stories about times they experienced particular feelings

Materials

- Agenda on chart paper or the chalkboard
- Chart paper for the feelings web
- Talking piece (a Hugg-A-Planet or an object with meaning to you and your students)

Gathering: A trip I'd like to take

Abbas goes on a long journey to find Mariama. Mariama goes on a journey to her new home. Issa also travels to the new home. What's a trip you'd like to take? Where would you like to go? It can be a short trip or a long trip.

Ask the students to talk with a partner for a minute or two. Then call on a couple of volunteers to share the trip they'd like to take.

Check agenda

Go over the objectives and the agenda.

Feelings web

Tell the students that you need their help to create a "feelings web." Write the word "feelings" in the middle of a piece of chart paper and draw a circle around it. Begin the web by asking the students to recall feelings experienced by the characters in the story. Record their responses. When they run out of ideas, you might remind them of events in the story that gave rise to feelings in the characters. Then see how many other feelings words your group can generate in a few minutes. Your web might start out looking something like this.

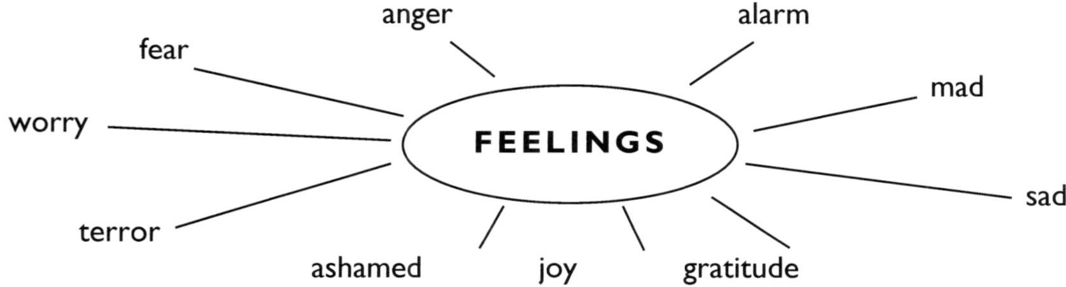

Tell the students that you'll keep the web and post it for each session. As feelings words come up in discussions, songs, poems, and stories throughout the school year, add those words to the web to build the students' feelings vocabularies.

Feelings charades

Ask, "Who has played charades before?" Explain that they're going to play a version of charades in which someone will pick a word from the feelings web and act out that feeling for the audience to guess it. In acting out the feeling, they can't make a sound. They have to express the feeling through facial expression, body language, gestures, or actions. Model the activity by picking a word and acting it out for the students to guess. Then give several volunteers a chance to act out a feeling for the group to guess.

"How can we tell what a person is feeling even if they don't tell us in words? Why is reading feelings in this way an important skill?" Call on a couple of volunteers to share their thoughts.

Stories about feelings

Explain that now you're going to ask the students to tell a story about a time they experienced a particular feeling. They can choose a feeling from the feelings web or another feeling. Model the activity by telling a brief story about a feeling you experienced. Where were you? What happened? What feeling did you experience? What did you do, if anything? How did it turn out? If possible, remember a feeling story from a time when you were the same age as they are.

Give students a couple of minutes to talk with a partner and share their stories. Then send the talking piece around for students to share their stories with the group.

Reflection/feedback and closing

Send the talking piece around for students to say one word that expresses how they're feeling right now.

Lesson 2

Objectives

Students will

- indicate how they're feeling on a "Feelings Barometer"
- define "anger trigger"
- identify their anger triggers and reflect on why people have the triggers they have
- practice a muscle relaxation technique to reduce tension.

Materials
- Agenda on chart paper
- Hugg-A-Planet or other soft object
- Copies of the "My Anger Triggers" for students (see handout at the end of the unit)
- Pencils
- Chart paper and markers
- A "Feelings Barometer" (a piece of chart paper with a horizontal line on top of which are numbers from -5 to +5, see below).
- Talking piece

Gathering: Name Game

Play the name game again, as in Unit 1. Have the students stand in a circle. Toss a Hugg-A-Planet or other soft object to a student. When the student catches it, s/he calls out her or his full name and then everyone yells, "Yes!" S/he then throws the ball to someone else, and so on around the circle till everyone has had a turn. Encourage students to pay close attention to who has the Hugg-A-Planet. How do you know when that person is ready to throw it? What can that person look for to know whether someone else is ready to receive it?

Check agenda

Go over the objectives and the agenda.

Feelings barometer

Explain that a barometer is an instrument that can help predict the weather by measuring air pressure in the atmosphere. Show them the feelings barometer. Explain that the feelings barometer can help us measure the emotional weather in the classroom.

Explain that in a minute you'll be asking students to come up and put an x under the number that best represents their overall feeling today. A –5 would be the worst way a student could be feeling. A +5 would be the best way a student could be feeling. Ask the students for reasons that might cause them to put an x under -5, or -2, or +3, and or +5.

Model the activity by putting an x under the number that represents how you're feeling and explain briefly why you're putting your x there. Ask whether there are any questions. Once the students understand how the feelings barometer works, have them come up in groups of three or four for each to put an x under the number that best represents how they're feeling right now. When all students are done, the feelings barometer might look something like this:

-5	-4	-3	-2	-1	0	+1	+2	+3	+4	+5
x		x	x	x	x		x	x		x
		x	x	x	x		x	x		
		x			x		x	x		

Without calling attention to any one student's x, ask for any general observations students want to make about the feelings barometer. Where do most of our feelings lie today? How does the group as a whole seem to be feeling? Is something going on in school that might explain the group's overall feeling—for example, a test or a basketball game with another school that everyone is looking forward to?

You can use the feelings barometer from time to time to gauge the emotional state of your group. You may want to keep and date the charts for comparison purposes.

Anger triggers

Explain that an anger trigger is an event or action that "pushes our buttons" provoking our anger.

Distribute copies of "My Anger Triggers" to the students (see handout at the end of the unit). Ask students to think of the kinds of things that make them angry and to list three of them on the handout. Ask students to number their anger triggers from 1 to 3, where 1 triggers them the most and 3 triggers them the least.

> **NOTE**: Ask students to write their names on their papers and collect them. You'll need them in Lesson 4.

Get students started by sharing some anger triggers of your own—for example: someone who cuts you off in traffic, things that aren't fair, rude people, people who don't clean up after themselves When students are done, send the talking piece around, asking each student to share an anger trigger. They should just name the trigger; there's no need for an explanation in this go-round. Students who do not wish to share should be allowed to pass.

Ask students what they notice about the triggers being shared. Why do they think that anger triggers can be different for different people? Something that triggers my anger may not trigger yours—and vice versa. Why do we have the triggers we have? Encourage students' thinking by sharing appropriate reflections about the origins of your own anger triggers.

Squeeze-Relax

As a transition from thinking about anger, ask students to tighten or squeeze the muscles in their feet, hold for three-five seconds, and then relax. Continue with legs, back, stomach, chest, hands, arms, shoulder, neck and face. Finish by asking students to squeeze all their muscles at the same time, hold for three to five seconds, and relax. Ask a few volunteers to describe what this was like.

Reflection/feedback and closing

Ask students to talk in pairs to share something they might do today to move their overall mood to a higher number on the feelings barometer. Model the activity by sharing what you might do to improve your overall mood. Give time for a couple of volunteers to share what they plan to do.

Lesson 3

Objectives

Students will
- learn that when they get angry, they have choices
- share stories about times they were angry
- identify constructive and destructive ways of dealing with anger
- identify "anger signals"--thoughts and bodily sensations that tell us we're angry
- brainstorm ways to cool down when we're angry

Materials

- Agenda on chart paper
- Talking piece
- Pencils
- Chart paper and markers
- T-chart with two columns, one marked "Constructive: What helps?" and the other marked "Destructive: What makes it worse?"

Gathering: Emotional weather check in

Ask students if they have ever heard people's moods described in the terms of weather. They might mention "stormy" or "sunny." Send the talking piece around the circle and ask students to give a brief description of their current emotional "weather" as if they were a weather forecaster, for example, cloudy with a chance of rain / blue skies continuing through the day / thunder and lightning / drizzle / sunny / hot & humid / gloomy / cool.

Check agenda

Review the objectives and agenda for the lesson

Anger choices

Explain that when we get angry, when our anger is triggered, we have choices. We can do things that the make the situation worse. Or, we can do things that make the situation better. Ask for a show of hands of students who can recall a time when they got angry and then did something that made the situation worse—for example, got them in trouble or led to a fight where someone got hurt. Call on a student or two to describe what happened.

Show the students the T-chart with the two columns: "Constructive: What helps?" and "Destructive: What makes it worse?" Explain that a "constructive" response is one that helps the people in a conflict work it out so both feel okay in the end. A "destructive" response is one that makes things worse and can lead to somebody getting hurt. Some kinds of responses may go in both columns; some won't fit in either. A response that helps in one situation may make things worse in another. Some responses may make people feel better but don't change the situation.

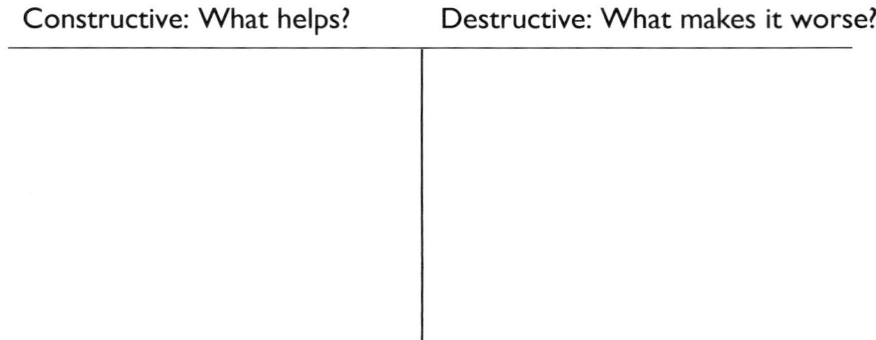

Anger stories

Explain that in a couple of minutes you're going to ask your students to pair up and talk with their partner about a time they were angry. They'll recall who was involved, what happened, what they did, and how it turned out. Was their way of dealing with the anger constructive or destructive?

Model the activity by telling them about a time you got angry, including what you did or didn't do, how it turned out, and whether you think your response was constructive or destructive. (It would be ideal if you can think of an anger story from when you were their age.) When you have finished your story, invite the class to take a deep breath with you.

Now it's their turn. Tell them you'd like one person to talk while the other listens actively. Each of them will have a minute and a half to talk while the other person listens. You'll keep the time and tell them when to switch. Suggest that partners take a deep breath together as each one finishes telling a story. If you think it's necessary, remind the students about confidentiality.

After the students are done talking in pairs, ask for a volunteer to share an experience of anger and to give an opinion about whether the response was constructive or destructive. The student should describe briefly what happened to trigger the anger, how they responded, and what happened next. Was their response helpful? Or did it make the situation worse? List the ways they responded in the appropriate column on the T-chart. Hear as many student stories as you have time for, each time engaging the student and the class in considering where the response should be placed on the chart.

Anger signals

Explain that an "anger signal" is what goes on in our bodies and our minds when we are angry.

Ask the students to think about the anger story they just told. Do they recall the sensations in their body that accompanied the anger? Call on a couple of students to share their thoughts.

If they have trouble recalling their anger signals, prompt them by sharing your anger signals. Or you might ask, Does your heart beat faster? Do you start to sweat? Do you feel blood rushing to your face? Is your mind filled with angry thoughts?"

Chart the anger signals you and the students come up with.

Point out that it's helpful to be aware of our anger signals so that we can control our anger instead of letting it control us. Sometimes anger can lead people to do things before they even have a chance to think. Knowing our anger signals can help us realize sooner that we're angry. That can give us time to make a conscious decision about the best thing to do in the situation.

Brainstorming ways to cool down

> **NOTE**: The aim of brainstorming is to get lots of ideas out in a short amount of time. The procedure for brainstorming is as follows: (1) Accept all ideas (without discussion of their pros and cons; (2) Give everyone a chance to contribute an idea before anyone gets to go twice; (3) Set a time limit of 3-5 minutes; (4) Use your imagination in thinking of ideas. Even ideas that seem unrealistic can sometimes be adapted in useful ways.

Explain that we all get angry sometimes. When our anger gets triggered, it's a good idea to pause, stop the action, and chill so that we can think more clearly about the smartest thing to do. Does this make sense? Why? Why not? Take some responses from students.

Lead the students in brainstorming ways they can cool down when their anger gets triggered.

As students share, write their ideas on a chart labeled "Ways to Cool Down." Their responses will probably include such time-tested strategies as counting to ten or taking a deep breath. When you finish, explain that these techniques are very helpful in the moment when you're angry. They can help you calm down so that you can think better. In the next lesson, students will learn two more ways to cool down.

Evaluation and closing: Weather report

Did the "weather" change for anyone during today's session? Ask a couple of volunteers to describe how the emotional weather changed for them and what caused the change.

Lesson 4

Objectives

Students will
- learn that "self-talk" can be a useful strategy for cooling down
- experience abdominal ("belly") breathing as a way to calm down and become more centered

Materials
- Agenda on chart paper or the chalkboard
- Filled-out "My Anger Triggers" handout from Lesson 2
- Balloon for abdominal breathing activity
- Construction paper and colored pencils, crayons, or markers for the optional activity "Drawing and Gallery Walk"
- Talking piece

Gathering

Send the talking piece around for students to say something they do to help them be more peaceful. It should be just one word that ends in –ing. Model the activity by sharing something you do, for example, listen<u>ing</u> (to music).

Check agenda

Go over the objectives and the agenda.

Self-Talk

Explain that one of the best strategies for calming yourself down is to talk to yourself. When something happens to trigger our anger, we can make ourselves angrier or calmer by what we say to ourselves.

For example, an adult yells at you. If you think to yourself, "No one treats me like that and gets away with it," you may make yourself angrier. But if you think something like, "S/he must be having a bad day, but s/he's not going to ruin mine by getting me in trouble," you're on the way to cooling down.

It's not okay for the person to treat you disrespectfully, but if you can calm yourself down, you may be able to think of a way to deal with the situation that stops the behavior you don't like and keeps you out of trouble.

Distribute the "My Anger Triggers" handout completed by the students in Lesson 2. Give them a couple of minutes to choose one of their anger triggers and think of a something they can say to themselves to calm themselves down when their anger is triggered in that way. Model the activity by sharing an example of self-talk you might use to deal with one of your anger triggers.

After the students have had time to think, send the talking piece around for students to share the anger trigger they have chosen and the simple sentence they might say to themselves so that they don't lose their cool when triggered.

Here are some typical examples of self-talk:
I won't let you ruin my day / This is not about me / I won't take the bait.

In self-talk, humor can be useful as well. You might say (to yourself) something absurd, like "Your donkey is wearing a purple polka dot bikini." Anything that makes you smile in your mind will lower the anger and be useful.

In conclusion, point out two crucial things to remember about self-talk:
- You say it in your mind, not out loud to the person who has triggered your anger
- Talking to yourself to cool down buys you some time to think about the best way to deal with the situation.

> **NOTE:** If you want to give the students more practice with self-talk, you can use the Self-Talk Work Sheet (see handout at the end of the unit) as the basis for an additional lesson.

*Abdominal Breathing**

Introduce the idea that deep breathing can help us relax and improve our thinking. In this activity, students will develop their skill in breathing deeply.

Ask your students to close their eyes and pay attention to their breathing. Are they breathing through their nose or through their mouth? Are their chests and bellies moving as they breathe? Call on several volunteers to share what they noticed.

Ask, Why do we breathe? Why is breathing important? Elicit or explain that our bodies need oxygen to release energy from the food we eat. Oxygen is an invisible gas in the air around us. When we breathe in, we bring oxygen into our lungs. From there our blood carries oxygen to all the parts of our body. When we breathe out, we expel gases that our body doesn't need.

Point out that most of the time we pay little attention to our breathing; we breathe without even thinking about it. This is a good thing. With our breathing going on automatically, we can go about our lives without having to focus on this essential life-giving process. But sometimes it's useful to pay attention to our breathing and breathe in a special way.

One special way of breathing is called abdominal breathing. Ask whether the students know what the abdomen is. Elicit or explain that it's a part of our body — our belly. Abdominal breathing is a special kind of breathing in which our belly expands (moves out) and then contracts (moves in) — and out and in, and out and in.

> **NOTE:** You can use a balloon to help students understand what goes on when we breathe. Blow the balloon up to half its capacity, let some air out, then blow it back up to half capacity. Explain that we have two lungs in our chest. When we breathe in, our lungs fill part way up with air. When we breathe out, they go down, or contract—like the balloon. When our breathing is shallow, our chest and lungs don't move very much.
>
> But if we breathe deeply, the lungs expand a lot. A muscle called the diaphragm, which is underneath the lungs and helps the lungs expand, pushes the organs in our abdomen down and out. So as our lungs expand to full capacity, our chest and belly expand too. Illustrate by blowing the balloon up to full capacity. Explain that as our lungs fill up with air and grow larger, the belly and the chest move out to make room for them.

Tell the students that you want them to try it. You'll show them how it's done. Put the palm of your hand on your abdomen. Breathe in deeply and slowly while expanding your belly and chest. Then breathe out slowly, contracting your belly. Ask the students what they noticed as they watched you. Elicit that you breathed slowly and that your hand—and your belly beneath it—moved out and in as you breathed.

Explain that you want them to do five cycles, each cycle consisting of one breath in and one breath out. Suggest that when they slowly breathe in (belly expanding), they can silently think, "In…" When they slowly breathe out (belly contracting), they can silently think, "Out…" Tell them to begin and do it with them. When you have done five cycles, ask, How was that for you? Was it easy to breathe in with your belly expanding and out with it contracting? How did it feel? Are there benefits to pausing sometimes to breathe this way? If they think so, what might they be? Elicit that abdominal breathing brings more oxygen into our lungs and helps us be healthy. Deep breathing also helps us relax and cool down. With more oxygen in our brains, we tend to think better.

Acknowledge that because abdominal breathing is a special kind of breathing, it takes practice. The more we do it, the more skilled we'll become.

* This activity is adapted from *Building Emotional Intelligence: Techniques to Cultivate Inner Strength in Children* by Linda Lantieri, pp. 74-76. The book is a great source of ideas for helping children relax their bodies and focus their minds.

Drawing and gallery walk (optional activity)

Distribute paper and drawing implements. Explain that for some people, thoughts, feelings, images, or sensations come up when they do abdominal breathing. Invite students to take five to ten minutes to draw what came up for them while they practiced abdominal breathing. These may be specific pictures, or more abstract ways of using color (the drawings do not have to be representational). Encourage students to consider what colors they want to use to express what this experience was like.

When students have finished drawing, invite them to leave the drawings on their desks, stand up, and circulate around the room to look briefly at each other's drawings. After the "Gallery Walk," invite them to share any observations about the drawings.

Evaluation and closing

Ask students to complete this sentence: A time or place in my life when I could use abdominal breathing is…

Lesson 5

Objectives

Students will
- learn and practice Plan 1-2-3 for centering themselves and thinking clearly about what to do when their anger is triggered

Materials

- Agenda on chart paper or the chalkboard
- Chart summarizing Plan 1-2-3
- Talking piece

Gathering

Give the students an opportunity to practice their breathing—and to calm and center themselves.

Turn off the lights and sit in a chair in front of the students. Ask them to do what you do. Put the palm of your hand on your abdomen. Breathe in deeply and slowly while expanding your belly and chest. Then breathe out slowly, contracting your belly.

Do five cycles, each cycle consisting of one breath in and one breath out. Remind them that when they slowly breathe in (belly expanding), they can silently think, "In…" When they slowly breathe out (belly contracting), they can silently think, "Out…"

With the lights still off, ask, How was that for you? Was it easy to breathe in with your belly expanding and out with it contracting? Did anything come into your mind as you were doing this? Did you find it relaxing?

Check agenda

Go over the objectives and the agenda.

Plan 1-2-3

We've shared strategies we use to cool down when we're angry, and we've learned about self-talk and abdominal breathing. Today we're going to learn another way to help us do the smartest thing when our anger gets triggered. It's called Plan 1-2-3 because it's as easy as 1, 2, 3.

Show them the chart of Plan 1-2-3 (below) and ask a volunteer to read the three steps.

1. Stop

2. Breathe

3. Think

Now say that you'll tell them more about each step of Plan 1-2-3. You want them to remember the three steps and what you say about them. They need to pay attention. After you've explained the three steps to them, you'll ask them to work in pairs to quiz each other on the steps.

Walk them through the steps, referring to the chart, and provide the following explanations:

Step 1 is to STOP yourself when you feel yourself getting upset <u>before you react</u>. Pay attention to your body and your mind. What are you thinking? What is your body saying to you? How are you feeling?

Step 2 is to BREATHE. Here's where abdominal breathing comes in. Take a few moments to breathe deeply — in and out, and in and out, and in and out, slowly. This will help you calm down a bit and think more clearly.

Step 3 is to THINK. After pausing and taking a few deep breaths, ask yourself, What is the smartest thing for me to do right now? Maybe the smartest thing is to do nothing. Maybe the smartest thing is to tell the other person how you're feeling in a strong but not mean way. We can be pretty sure that hitting or saying mean things is NOT the smartest thing to do. Think of your choices. Think of the consequences.

Tell the students that as our year with The 4Rs goes on, they will be learning that they have choices when they're angry or scared or in conflict. They'll explore the consequences of various actions. That will increase their skill in using Plan 1-2-3.
Now ask students to pair up and quiz each other on the steps. They should ask each other to say the three steps and give an explanation of each.

After students have had a few minutes to work in pairs, cover the chart of Plan 1-2-3 and call on a couple of volunteers to recite the three steps and describe what's involved in each.

Now it's time to practice Plan 1-2-3.

Practicing Plan 1-2-3

Ask the students to form two lines facing each other so that each person has a partner. If you have an odd number of students, you will be someone's partner. Ask the students to shake hands with their partners.

Explain that they will be "thought partners," putting their heads together to think of creative ways to deal with situations that trigger their anger. You are going to describe a situation in which students' anger might be triggered, and take the students through the steps of Plan 1-2-3 to deal with it.

Use a situation of your own devising or choose one from the list in the box below. Here are steps you might follow:

- Describe the situation to the students

- Ask them to imagine themselves in this situation—that it is really happening to them. Ask students to give you a thumbs-up when they are picturing themselves in the situation.

- Now it's time for Plan 1-2-3. Ask, What's Step 1? Okay, let's do it. STOP and imagine how you'd be feeling. What would be going through your mind? What would be going on in your body? Call on several volunteers to share.

- What is Step 2? Okay, let's all BREATHE together. Lead them in taking a couple of deep breaths.

- What's Step 3? Okay, take a couple of minutes to THINK with your partner about what would be the smartest thing to do in this situation.

- Call on pairs of students to share the ideas they came up with. After one pair shares, ask whether other students agree with their approach. Encourage lively discussion back and forth. Accept students' ideas without judgment. The most important thing we're going for here is that the students are <u>thinking</u> about the best thing to do in these situations. As the year goes on and students learn more skills, they will see more possibilities and be better able to evaluate their options.

Repeat this procedure with other situations.

Situations for Practicing Plan 1-2-3

- You ask your parents to buy you new sneakers like the ones that a number of kids in your class are wearing. They say, "No way!"

- Your uncle promised to take you to the movies for your birthday. You wait for him to pick you up after school, but he doesn't show. Later you get a text from him saying, "Something came up. We'll do it another time."

- You and your older sister/brother have always been close. You used to hang out and have fun doing things together. But now that s/he's in high school, you hardly ever see him/her. S/he agrees to go to the park with you on Saturday, but s/he forgets and goes off with her friends.

<hr>

Situations for Practicing Plan 1-2-3 *continued*

- You're on your school's basketball team. You get into an argument with one of your teammates, and other players have to separate the two of you to prevent a fight. The coach (who is one of your favorite teachers) benches both of you. You will both have to sit out the next game—and it's a big game with the school's arch rival.

- You make plans to hang out with your favorite cousin on the weekend, but your mother says, "You can't go till you clean your room and help me with the laundry."

- You and your best friend have your desks next to each other in the classroom. Your teacher informs you that s/he's splitting the two of you up, moving you and your desk to another cluster, because you and your friend spend too much time talking and too little time working.

- A school aide makes your whole class sit out recess because a couple of your classmates were acting up during lunch.

- You tried out for a lead in a school play. You got a small part, but not the lead part you wanted. You had worked hard to prepare for the audition and were sure you had done well. You believe that the person who got the part is a "teacher's pet."

<hr>

Evaluation and Closing

Back in the circle, send the talking piece around for students to share their thoughts about Plan 1-2-3. Can they see themselves using it in real life? Why? Why not?

End with a round of applause for their hard work on this challenging topic.

<u>Additional Activities</u>

Blind Drawing

As Issa lost his sight, Mariama had to learn to describe what she saw in great detail: "So now Mariama had another skill to learn: how to use words to show Issa the things that his eyes could not see." Ask the class to experience what this is like by having them form pairs and sit back to back. One person in the pair is given a simple picture (magazine pictures can be used); the other is given paper and drawing materials (crayons, markers, colored pencils). The person who is holding the picture must describe it to their partner, without showing it. The partner tries to draw the picture from the description. After 5 minutes or so, allow the partners to compare the pictures. Reverse roles. Discuss what made this easy or difficult. What is it like to use words to show someone things they cannot see?

Write about something you value

Research** shows that a simple intervention can boost the confidence of African-American and Latino students and improve their academic performance. Social pychologists Geoffrey Cohen, Jonathan Cook, and Valerie Purdie-Vaughns found that 7th and 8th grade African-American and Latino students who completed a simple "values affirmation exercise" several times during the school year showed significant improvement in grades and test scores compared with students of similar backgrounds who didn't do the exercise.

The exercise was simple: The students were asked to write for 15 minutes about something that mattered deeply to them (e.g. religion, family, an extracurricular pursuit).

Consider the findings of this research when assigning writing topics, especially around standardized-testing time.

*Reported in *New York Magazine*, "Simple Way to Boost Minority Test Scores," Jennifer Senior, August 9, 2013

What is peace?

Write the word "peace" in the middle of a piece of chart paper and draw a circle around it. Ask the students what comes to mind when they think of peace. Record their responses, creating a web. You are collecting their free associations. There are no wrong answers. Add your free associations as well. Your web might look something like this:

Ask the students how they would define the word "peace." Elicit that peace is a state of happiness and well-being, free of violence and hurting. We often think of peace as being quiet or calm, but it doesn't have to be. Peace can be exciting and fun. But it's a time when you are in harmony with yourself and others.

Draw a peaceful place

Ask the students to close their eyes and recall a place they went or something they did that was peaceful. For Issa and Mariama, it is the desert. For Abbas, it is his father's palace. Later, Issa and Mariama will grow to love the garden in the palace. Model thinking of such a place for the students by sharing your memory of a peaceful time or place. Maybe it was a picnic with your family by a beautiful pond when everyone had a great time. Maybe it was a walk by yourself in the park. Give your students a minute or two to think of their own peaceful time or place. Ask them to give you a "thumbs-up" when they have thought of something. Encourage students who haven't thought of something yet. Tell them that if a memory of a peaceful time or place is not coming to mind, they can try to imagine a place they could go or something they could do that would be peaceful.

Distribute crayons and drawing paper and explain that you want them to create an art work that expresses their peaceful place or time. It might be a drawing that shows the place or the activity. Or it might be a design that expresses how they feel in their peaceful place or activity. They should leave room at the bottom of the paper for a sentence or two of explanation.

When they've completed their art works and captions, ask them to pair up and present their work to their partners. Ask a couple of volunteers to share with the group.

Post their completed work on a bulletin board or on the wall above your Peace Corner. (See below.)

Cloudy and Clear

A useful visual aid for explaining how abdominal breathing can help settle the mind can be made with a clear plastic jar, spoon, water, and clean sand. Show the class a clear jar full of water and ask if they can see to the other side. Then pour in some sand, and stir vigorously with a spoon. Ask the students if they can see to the other side of the jar now; while the sand is stirred up, the water will become cloudy, making it impossible to see through the jar. Then ask students to watch while the sand gradually settles to the bottom of the jar. Ask what they notice – they will likely say that the water is now clear again. Explain that the thoughts and feelings that fill our minds, especially when we are angry or afraid, can be like the sand in the water; they can make it hard to think clearly. Abdominal breathing can help our thoughts and feelings to "settle down", so that we can think clearly and be more aware of what is happening inside and around us.

This can also be demonstrated with a snow globe or other similar objects.

Create a Peace Corner in your classroom

Explain that you want the students' help in making a place in the classroom where they can go for a few minutes to relax if they are upset about something. <u>The Peace Corner will not be a place where a student is sent for a "time out." Going to the Peace Corner will be completely voluntary.</u> A good book for introducing students to the idea of a Peace Corner is *A Quiet Place* by Douglas Wood.

Have a space in mind that you and the class can turn into a little nook with a clear identity, distinct from the rest of the classroom. It should include a small table or desk and a blank wall above the desk that can be decorated with children's art. On the wall above the desk should be a beautiful sign, made by students, naming the space as the "Peace Corner."

Have the class brainstorm ideas of what might go into the Peace Corner: for example, paper and pencils for writing, crayons and paper for drawing, books about feelings, coloring books, a Hugg-A-Planet, a chart with the steps of Plan 1-2-3, photos of beautiful things from nature.

Involve the class in making ground rules for the use of the Peace Corner, for example,
- Ask the teacher's permission to go to the Peace Corner
- Return to your regular classroom activities as soon as you feel ready
- Take yourself to a peaceful place in your mind
- Use Plan 1-2-3 to cool yourself down

With the students' help, set up the Peace Corner and see how it goes!

Set aside time for silence and breathing

The school day is hectic and stressful for students and teachers. It's useful to build in time each day for a few minutes of silence. During this time the lights are off. No writing, drawing, reading. Just sitting. Students can close their eyes if they want. You can tell them that they can let their minds use the silence as they wish. Or you can suggest ways they might use the silence. For example, to

- practice abdominal breathing.
- pay attention to their breathing
- pay attention to sounds they hear
- take themselves to a peaceful place in their mind
- recall a time they had fun
- recall something they like to do

Be sure to take this opportunity to enjoy a couple of minutes of silence yourself.

Make "time for silence" part of your daily routine. You might carve out a few minutes for silence when the students come back from lunch and recess, or at the beginning or end of the day as well as after lunch.

A few minutes of silence at strategic times during the day will pay off in a calmer, more focused class. And you'll be developing in your students a habit and skill that will serve them well throughout their lives.

"I Whistle a Happy Tune"

It's an old song, but you and your students may like it. Ask students to raise their hands if they're willing to admit that they've been scared about something at one time or other in their lives. Ask a couple of volunteers to name what they were afraid of.

Ask, What are things you do when you're afraid? Call on a couple of volunteers to share what they do.

Say that you'll teach them a famous song that has ideas about what you can do when you're afraid. Use your phone or a computer to find "I Whistle a Happy Tune" on YouTube and play it for your students. (See handout at the end of the unit for the lyrics).

After introducing the song to the students, ask how they feel about whistling a happy tune when they're afraid. Do they think that would work for them? How about humming a happy tune?

Once students have learned the words to the song, they can add facial expressions and body postures to act out some of the feelings mentioned in the song ("afraid," "I hold my head erect," "shivering in my shoes," "a careless pose," "happiness," "brave"). Does changing your facial expression or posture change how you feel?

Consider having your students keep a 4Rs journal

Writing (drawing for younger students) is an excellent way to reinforce and consolidate learning. A journal enables students to put all of their Book Talk writing in one place. You can also give them a few minutes after each 4Rs lesson to jot down a few thoughts about what they're taking away or how they're planning to use what they've just learned. If a student tries a new skill, s/he might want to write about what happened. Did it bring a positive result? If a student is stuck in a conflict with someone, s/he might want to do some writing to sort it out and imagine some solutions. You can give them standard journals and encourage them to decorate them.

By having students keep journals, you will be introducing them to a habit or practice that can serve them well the rest of their lives.

Related Books

Cloud Tea Monkeys by Mal Peet and Elspeth Graham, illustrated by Juan Wijngarrd (picture book with quest theme)

Bridge to Terabithia; Celia and the Sweet, Sweet Water; The Great Gilly Hopkins; Park's Quest; and *The Sign of the Chrysanthemum* by Katherine Paterson. These are quest books dealing with a child's search for a parent, a cure for a parent's illness, or for knowledge about a parent.

Walk Two Moons, by Sharon Creech

A Quiet Place, by Douglas Wood

Handout 1 • Unit 2

Name ___________________________

My Anger Triggers

Think of the kinds of things that make you angry. List three of them below, with Number 1 being what triggers you the most and Number 3 what triggers you the least.

1. ____

____

____

2. ____

____

3. ____

____

Handout 2 ◆ Unit 2

Self-Talk Work Sheet

Look at your anger triggers from Lesson 3 of this unit. Complete this worksheet as in the sample provided below.

1. Anger trigger: *Getting blamed for something I didn't do.*

Specific situation: *My mother yells at me for starting a fight with my younger brother when he was the one who started it.*

Self-talk to calm myself down: *I'm not going to lose control here. I refuse to give my brother the satisfaction.*

2. Anger trigger: ____

Specific situation: ____

____

____

Self-talk to calm myself down: ____

____

____

3. Anger trigger: ____

Specific situation: ____

____

____

Self-talk to calm myself down: ____

____

____

Handout 3 ◆ Unit 2

"I Whistle a Happy Tune"
from *The King and I* by Richard Rodgers and Oscar Hammerstein II

"Whenever I feel afraid
I hold my head erect
        And whistle a happy tune,
So no one will suspect
I'm afraid.

While shivering in my shoes
I strike a careless pose
And whistle a happy tune,
And no one ever knows
I'm afraid.

The result of this deception
Is very strange to tell,
For when I fool the people I fear
I fool myself as well!

I whistle a happy tune,
And every single time
The happiness in the tune
Convinces me that I'm
Not afraid!

Make believe you're brave
And the trick will take you far;
You may be as brave
As you make believe you are.
You may be as brave
As you make believe you are."

Blank by design.

5

Unit 3 Theme

Becoming a Better Listener

Unit 3 Book Selection

Encounter by Jane Yolen
Voyager Books, Harcourt Brace & Company, 1992

Activities

- Intro to Active Listening: The Three Ps
- The First P: Paying Good Attention
- The Second P: Providing Gentle Encouragement
- The Third P: Paraphrasing
- Introducing the Concept of Conflict
- Writing about Conflict
- Point of View: Young Woman / Old Woman
- Role-play on Point of View
- Additional Activities

Introduction

Therapists call it "listening with the third ear"; folk adages warn that children "learn from what you do, not what you say," or that "Actions speak louder than words"; Native Americans urge that we not judge another until we have walked in that person's moccasins. No matter how you say it, the message is clear. Communication is more than one person speaking and another listening. Two people may hear the same words, but each understands them through filters of culture and experience. In addition, tone of voice, body language, what is said or not said give information about what people are thinking and feeling.

The ability to listen well and to understand another person's point of view is crucial to social and emotional learning. In any human interaction (and, by extension, any conflict) each person has his or her own point of view. I can like chocolate ice cream and you can like vanilla, but if my point of view is that people who like vanilla have no taste we could end up in conflict. Many people make the mistake of thinking that their point of view is the norm and, therefore, that the solution to any conflict with another will involve that person or group coming around to their point of view. In fact, if there is a solution, it lies in finding common ground, not in changing deeply held beliefs or cultural conditioning.

Before we can understand another's point of view, we must be good listeners. A good listener takes in information, interprets it, draws conclusions about what the person is saying, and uses all this to try to understand what is going on.

Being able to put one's own mind into another's as much as possible makes for better listening. The better the listening, the more accurate the analysis and the more useful the response.

One could argue that listening well to people is the key to social and emotional learning.

GOOD LISTENING

- shows respect for (and interest in) the other person
- helps avoid misunderstanding
- helps clear up misunderstandings if they occur
- gives us important information about how the other person is thinking and feeling
- can help defuse anger
- can help us develop and improve our thinking

COMMUNICATION BARRIERS INCLUDE

- blaming the other person
- using put-downs
- ignoring the other person's concerns
- offering solutions too early
- not taking the other person's concerns seriously
- thinking only of our own ideas
- interrupting

Listening is a skill that can be learned. We assume not only that good listening is essential in dealing well with conflict, but that we can all improve our skills and become better listeners. Although listening is part of every unit, it is the special focus of this unit.

Students at all grade levels practice a set of skills called "active listening." Active listening has three main components: paying good attention, providing gentle encouragement (to the speaker), and restating or reflecting to the speaker what we've heard (to show our interest and check our understanding).

We also help students to understand the concept of point of view and its relationship to literature and to social and emotional learning. It is because each of us has a point of view that good listening is so critical. We can't assume that others see things as we do. If we truly want to respect other people, we often have to work hard to understand where they're coming from.

GOOD LISTENING CHECKLIST

- Positive body language
- Eye contact
- No interrupting

In this unit

	Ideas	Skills
Literacy	• Every character has a point of view • Objects in a story can stand for a feeling or thought; they are symbols • Symbols can foreshadow the action in a story • History is usually written by the "winners," but the "losers" also have a history	• Predicting • Identifying the main idea • Asking questions • Expressing ideas clearly • Providing evidence to back up one's assertions • Listening
Social and Emotional Learning	• The same facts appear to be different to different people • Culture determines much of our point of view	• The 3 Ps of Active listening: • Paying good attention • Providing gentle encouragement • Paraphrasing • Understanding body language • Defining conflict • Understanding another person's point of view • Brainstorming solutions

Encounter, by Jane Yolen, illus. by David Shannon. Voyager Books, Harcourt Brace & Company, 1992.

SUMMARY

A young Taino boy wakes from a dream of three white birds on the sea. Their teeth are menacing. He goes to the shore and finds three "great-sailed canoes. . . .[that] gave birth to many little ones that swam awkwardly to our shore." "All dreams are not true dreams, my mother says," but his every instinct warns him against the strange beings. "'Do not welcome them,' I begged the chief. 'My dream is a warning.'" But "it is our custom to welcome strangers" and because he is a child the chief dismisses his qualms: "'All children have bad dreams.'"

The baby canoes "spat out many strange creatures, men but not men." These creatures cover their bodies in bright colors "like parrots" and no one can see their feet. "'We must see if they are true men,'" says the chief. "So I took one by the hand and pinched it. The hand felt like flesh and blood, but the skin was moon to my sun." The chief determines that no one that pale can come from the earth: "'Surely they come from the sky.'" The two peoples exchange gifts. The strangers have items that the Taino people covet--swords, mirrors, guns--but they give only beads, hats, and bells. The strangers covet the gold that the Tainos wear, but they receive only balls of cotton thread, fish spears, parrots, and rubber balls. The boy seeks counsel from his zemis, but the zemis was silent, it "spoke only in dreams. Indeed, it had spoken to me already." The boy's sense of foreboding increases. The next day, the strangers return to their great canoes, taking five young men and the narrator with them. At the first opportunity, the narrator slips overboard and returns to shore. He is now far from home, and as he walks, "following the sun," he meets other people: "I told of the pale strangers from the sky. I said our blood would cry out in the sand. I spoke of my dream of the white teeth. But even those who saw the great canoes did not listen, for I was a child."

And so it was, he comments, that "we lost our lands to the strangers from the sky." Still, he, "an old man now," who dreams "no more dreams," continues to tell the story. "May it be a warning to all the children and all the people in every land."

COMMENT

This deceptively simple story is rich in literary and historical content. It has layers of historical references that can be uncovered depending on the background information that the students have or their desire to explore the period more.

Until recently, stories of the first encounters of Europeans with indigenous people were told from the point of view of the Europeans. We have Christopher Columbus's journals. We do not have any record of what the Taino thought. The writer has taken the point of view both of an indigenous person and a child to imagine what that point of view might have been. This point of view is still not widely acknowledged by the dominant culture and this story may be the first time that students have heard it. We know that the victors write history, a concept that the students may not know but that again illustrates point of view. In this case, the conquerors destroyed whatever written records existed of indigenous peoples, so that we know very little of the civilizations in what is now called Central and Latin America and the Caribbean. We do know from the writings of the Europeans what happened to the people who were there at the time of the Encounter.

As we look at this story, we can focus on the writer's vivid imagery and symbolism. One of the most striking aspects of the writing is the way that the narrator describes items that may be familiar to all of us raised in a modern western culture. Through his eyes we see them for the first time. We enter into his point of view. We notice the body language of the strangers, whose words we do not understand. We hear the harshness in their voices, see the coldness in their eyes. We feel his frustration at not being believed because he is a child.

And we see the beginnings of a conflict that ended in disaster and annihilation for one side. We have to infer the point of view of the pale ones. We can read it elsewhere. They, too, thought they were dealing with non-humans. They, too, had dreams and visions.

Book Talk

READ-ALOUD

Previewing the book

Ask first what the word "encounter" means. Then show the cover of the book and ask students to guess who may be involved in the encounter.

Reading and responding to the book

Read the story.

After you have read the story, ask the students to pair up and talk about the book. What interests them? What questions do they have? Ask students to share their questions and comments with the class. Encourage as much class participation as possible by asking follow-up questions and asking students to back up their assertions with examples from the book.

At some point the questions may lead to a discussion of Columbus. If they don't, make the link, share information, perhaps reading from the author's description of why she wrote the book.

Ask whether any students have read other books about Christopher Columbus or about the Tainos. What point of view did those books have?

Deepening students' understanding of the book

Ask the students to re-tell the story. What happened? How do we know what happened? Who tells us what happened? Get as many ideas as possible. In this unit, our focus is on point of view. Introduce the concept of point of view. Each character in a story has a point of view. This particular story is written from one person's point of view and is told as a first-person narrative (*The Keeping Quilt* was also a first-person narrative).

Say that you will read the book again. This time you want the students to look at how the author communicates point of view and listening. Pay attention also to the way that the illustrator reinforces that point of view. You will be looking at how the drawings are from a child-size perspective, how the descriptions convey the newness of the items to the narrator, what aspects of the encounter the narrator emphasizes.

Explain that there are many ways of listening. We listen to our bodies when we are hungry, we listen to the tone of voice in people who speak to us and we interpret those tones, we observe body language. In this story, there are people who do not speak each other's language, yet they are communicating. What do we think they are communicating? Ask students to raise their hands when they notice listening or non-listening happening. Push for examples, such as the boy listening to his dream, how the strangers touched their gold but not their flesh (body language), how his zemis spoke to him, how the blood cried out but "no one heard."

When you reach the parts where the strangers' gifts are described, be sure that the students understand what the gifts are.

Ask students to give examples of symbolism in the book. What do the birds symbolize? What is symbolized by the boy's cutting his hand on the sword? What do the flags that the pale ones put in the ground symbolize? Elicit as many interpretations as the students offer.

Connecting the book to students' lives

Discussion: Has there ever been a time when someone didn't listen to you because you are a child? Have you ever misunderstood something that was happening because you didn't have enough information about it? Pair up and talk about it with a partner.

This story takes place in the Caribbean, but a similar story took place in what we now call North America. However, we have reason to believe that the very first Europeans who came by sea, the Vikings, did not come back. They did not have guns and they may have suffered in battles with the people who were already here. Can we imagine a story in which the Europeans did not stay? What would life in this country be like now?

Writing: Find a common classroom object that would have been unthinkable a hundred years ago and ask students to write a description of it without using modern words (computer, ball point pen, calculator, stickers, paperback books, etc.).

Remind students of the descriptions of the objects brought by the strangers: "the sharp silver spear; round pools to hold in the hand that gave a man back his face; darts that sprang from sticks with a sound like thunder that could kill a parrot many paces away." (p. 20) Think about the first time you ever saw something that you now think is very common (a cement mixer, a cell phone, the ocean, a mountain, very, very tall building, a person with a skin color different from yours, an elephant). How old were you? Can you remember what your first thoughts were? Write them down using descriptive language that a person unfamiliar with that object might use. Try to capture the essence of what that object looks like, using comparisons to familiar objects as the book's narrator does.

Make three columns, one for the narrator, one for the Taino, and one for the Europeans. In each column, list the point of view of that person or group; i.e., the boy wants to repel the newcomers, the Taino want to be hospitable, the Europeans want to find gold. Write a story about one of the characters, using the information you have about point of view. What do you understand now about why the character acted as he or she did? Is there anything you would like to change in the story?

ROLE-PLAY

Ask students to act out the scene where the strangers put sticks in the ground. What were they actually doing? How do we know this? Is there any way that the Tainos could have known it? Students should invent dialogue for the strangers and for the Tainos. Ask some students to act out the scene where the chief raises his hands in the air to show the strangers that he recognizes that they have come from the sky. Again, they should invent dialogue, imagining what the strangers might be saying and what the Tainos might be saying. What do you think that the pale strangers thought the chief meant?

Applied Learning

SOCIAL AND EMOTIONAL LEARNING LESSONS

<u>Lesson I</u>

Objectives

Students will

- learn and practice a simple classroom ritual for good listening;
- identify the "Three Ps" of Active Listening;
- practice the first "P": paying good attention;
- practice the second "P": providing gentle encouragement.

Materials

- Agenda on chart paper or the chalkboard
- Hugg-A-Planet or other soft object to use as a talking piece
- A piece of chart paper with the heading "Good Listening Dos"

Gathering: Favorite Color

What's your favorite color? Each student takes a turn to answer this question in the following way: "My name is ____________ and my favorite color is ____________."

When everyone takes a turn speaking, we call it a "go-round." Take the opportunity of today's go-round to introduce (or re-introduce) a simple classroom ritual for talking and listening. You can use an object like a Hugg-A-Planet or other soft object as a "talking piece." The student who is speaking holds the object. Only the person holding it can speak, while all of the others give that person their full attention.

Check agenda

Go over the objectives and the agenda.

Introduction to active listening: The Three Ps

To respect other people, we need to understand where they're coming from. Our natural tendency is to assume that other people see things the way we do. But we can't assume this. Two people can see the same situation very differently. To work well with others, to solve conflicts and problems, we have to understand how the other person sees things and what s/he wants or is hoping for. Because we can't assume they see things as we do and because we can't read people's minds, we have to listen.

Many unnecessary conflicts can be avoided if people listen well, treat each other with respect, and try to understand where the other person is coming from. When we have a conflict, listening is one of the best ways to work toward a solution. We are listening all time—we listen to television, to noise on the street, to people talking. One of our goals in this class is to learn and practice a special kind of listening called "active listening." To help the students remember the skills that make up active listening, we can say that it consists of

The Three Ps
Paying good attention
Providing gentle encouragement
Paraphrasing and reflecting back what we hear

By practicing the Three Ps, we show respect for other people, we learn from them, we understand where they are coming from.

The First P: Paying good attention

Say that in this activity, we'll review "Good and Poor Listening" (introduced in Unit 1) and create a list of listening Dos. We'll focus especially on the "First P," paying good attention.

Ask for a volunteer to come up and talk about something s/he likes to do. Model paying good attention and ask the students to watch you closely. After the student is done talking, ask the students to identify specific behaviors of yours that represented paying good attention (for example, you were facing the student, you sat down so you were more at eye level, you had a smile on your face, you looked right at the student). Record those behaviors on a chart of Good Listening Dos.

Ask the students to pair up. One student speaks for one minute about something s/he likes to do on the weekend while the other student gives good attention (by showing good listening behaviors). Then they switch roles and the talker now listens attentively.

Afterward, discuss: How did it feel when someone paid good attention to you? How was it to be the listener? Easy? Difficult? All of us, no matter our age, need reminders to keep our listening at its best. So give the students ample opportunities to practice paying good attention, one of the key aspects of active listening.

The Second P: Providing gentle encouragement

Tell the students that another part of active listening, the "Second P," is providing gentle encouragement. You can do this by simply saying, "Tell me more" or "I'd like to hear more about that." You can also ask questions. When you ask a question, you show you're interested in what the other person is saying. We often ask questions when we don't understand something or when we want to know more. In school, if you don't understand something the teacher says, it's important to ask a question. If you don't, you may miss some important directions or some important information.

To illustrate the skill, talk about something that happened to you recently and pause to encourage the students to ask you a question about your story—either something they want to know more about or something they don't understand. Reverse roles: Ask a student to come up and talk about a favorite pet and model asking gentle questions to get the person to say more.

Then ask the children to talk in pairs about a favorite pet or their favorite animal and say that in this exercise, in addition to paying good attention, you want them to ask a question of the other person. Remind the class about the Abdominal Breathing technique that they learned in Unit 2. Taking a few deep breaths often helps the speaker to be clearer about what they want to say, and helps the listener to focus and give good attention to the speaker. Ask them to take three abdominal breaths together before beginning. After the first student has had a turn to talk and answer the other student's question, they switch and the other student gets a chance to talk.

Evaluation

What's one thing you learned today about one of your classmates that you didn't know before? Remind the students to ask their share partners whether it is ok to share that information. Give several volunteers a chance to tell the class.

Closing: Moment of silence

Tell the students you want them to close their eyes and become completely still. When they are completely quiet, you want them to listen very well. Do they hear anything? If so, what are the sounds? Where are they coming from?

After a minute or two of "silence," ask them what sounds, if any, they heard. What do they think was making each of the sounds they heard? Why do they think so?

Lesson 2

Objectives

Students will
- practice the skill of paraphrasing;
- practice the skill of reflecting feelings.

Materials

- Agenda on chart paper or the chalkboard

Gathering: Something new in our lives

In *Encounter*, two groups of people meet each other for the first time. Think about a time when a new being—a friend, a baby brother or sister, a step parent, a pet—came into your life. What was the experience like for you? Did it change you?

Give the students a chance to talk for a few minutes in pairs, then ask a couple of volunteers to share with the group.

Check agenda

Go over the objectives and the agenda.

The Third P: Paraphrasing

Tell the students that another part of active listening, the "Third P," is paraphrasing: saying back in your own words what someone has said. Model it by asking for a volunteer to come up and talk about his or her favorite sport or game. After the student has spoken for a

minute or so, paraphrase what the student said. Ask the student whether you have it right.
Then reverse roles and ask the student to paraphrase what you say.

Then give the students a chance to practice in pairs. Keep the time for them: one minute for
the speaker to talk while the listener listens; another minute or so for the listener to
paraphrase; another minute or less for the speaker to correct the paraphrase or add anything
s/he wants to add. After the exercise is finished, ask the listeners how it was to listen and
paraphrase. Was it easy? Difficult? If so, how? Then ask the speakers how they felt having
someone pay good attention and then paraphrase what they'd said. Point out that
paraphrasing is a key skill in mediation — where a third person helps two disputants talk out
a conflict they're having. (Students may be familiar with mediation if they have a peer
mediation program in their school.)

Evaluation

What's one thing you learned from today's lesson?

Closing: New Millennium Telephone Game

Begin with the traditional game in which you whisper a sentence to the student next to you
who whispers it to the next person and so on all around the circle. Do it once in the
traditional way. Then tell the students you'll play the game again, but this time they should
use active listening. In other words, they should pay good attention, ask a question if they
aren't sure they've heard correctly, and restate (in a whisper) what they've heard to be sure
they got it. The message should come through much better this time.

Lesson 3

Objectives

Students will
- define the word "conflict"
- share times that they were involved in a conflict
- write about conflicts

Materials

- Agenda on chart paper or the chalkboard
- Paper and pencil for writing

Gathering: Who's the Leader?

The class is sitting in a circle. One student leaves the room. While s/he is gone, choose a
student to be the leader. The leader's role is to do a series of things with his or her hands
(clapping, snapping fingers, slapping knees, etc.), changing from one thing to another
without stopping. The rest of the class follows the leader, immediately imitating the
motions. With the one student out of the room, the leader and the class begin. Then the

student is called back into the room and has to figure out, through sharp observation, who the leader is. Of course, the leader and the class are trying just as hard to switch seamlessly from one motion to another so that it's hard to tell who the leader is.

Check agenda

Go over the objectives and the agenda.

Introducing the concept of conflict

Encounter presents the historical conflict between the Spanish and the Tainos by portraying Columbus's first visit to a Caribbean island (called Guanahani by the indigenous people and San Salvador by the Spanish). The conflict was an extremely complex one, involving deep cultural differences, historical forces that go far beyond the characters and their interactions in the story, and realities of power. We should avoid simplistic explorations of the issues in the conflict (for example, by having students role-play a win-win solution to the conflict achieved by active listening!). But with that caveat, we can begin to examine some of the ideas and issues the book presents. One of them is the concept of conflict. The book speaks of the larger conflict between the Spanish and Tainos over land, cultural values, and sheer survival. It also shows a conflict between Taino adults in the story and the young boy, who sees more clearly the dangers and tries unsuccessfully to warn them.

Write the word conflict in the middle of the chalkboard or a large piece of chart paper. What does the word mean? Elicit that it's an argument, a disagreement, a dispute. Ask what conflicts they recall from the story. Then ask the students to say words that come to their minds when they hear the word "conflict." Write the words on the board or chart paper and connect them with lines to the word "conflict" to form a web. Below is a typical "conflict web."

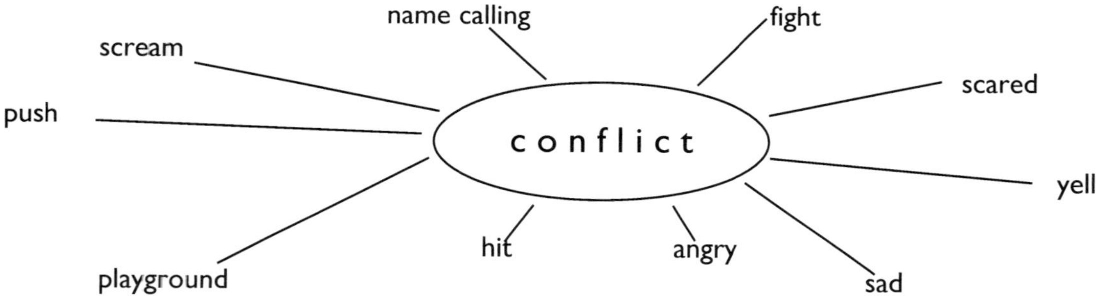

Ask the students if they have anything they want to say about the web. What do they notice? Most conflict webs, whether made by young people or adults, consist primarily of negative words. The students may notice this. If they don't (and if it's true of your web), point it out. Explain that people often see conflict as something bad because they tend to link it with violence, with people hurting other people. Conflict can lead to violence sometimes, but it doesn't have to, especially if people have the skills we're developing through The 4Rs curriculum.

There are many kinds of conflicts. Friends can argue over what they want to do together during free time. Classmates can argue over who gets to go first on the computer. Teachers can have conflicts with students. Children can have conflicts with their parents. Large groups of people, including whole countries, can have conflicts with other groups. This is normal. We all have conflicts from time to time. Conflict is part of life. Ask students to work in pairs, taking a minute or two each to share stories of a recent conflict they were part of or witnessed. After the students have talked in pairs, ask for several volunteers to share their stories with the class. Discuss: What happened? How did the conflict turn out? Were you happy with the way you handled it?

Writing about conflict

Once you're sure the class understands the concept, have them do a writing activity. Ask them to write about a time they had a conflict. Suggest that their pieces include the following (not necessarily in this order):

- Who was involved in the conflict?
- Where did it take place?
- How were you feeling? How were other people feeling? How did you and the other people express their feelings?
- What caused the conflict?
- What happened? How did it turn out? Was the conflict resolved?
- Were you happy with the way it came out?

Give the students 20-30 minutes to write a draft, then ask them to share their writing with a partner. It's OK if they aren't done with their piece. They can read what they've written and tell the rest of the story. Remind them to use their good listening skills in paying attention to the other person's piece. They should feel free to use the Second P (Provide Gentle Encouragement) if they want to know more.

After the students have read their pieces to each other in pairs, ask for several volunteers to read their pieces to the group.

Discuss: Was it helpful to write about a conflict? Did writing lead to any insights that will help you deal with this conflict or with a similar conflict in the future?

Evaluation

What's one new idea that you're taking away from this lesson? Give several volunteers a chance to share their thoughts.

Closing: Clap and Repeat

Clap out a simple rhythm, or tap a rhythm on a small drum. Ask the students to respond by clapping out the same rhythm in unison. Clap out another rhythm for students to imitate and then another and another. As the activity progresses, rhythms may become longer and more complex. Students can also be invited to take turns leading the "Clap and Repeat". Continue for as long as interest remains high. This builds listening skills, and a sense of community.

Ask students: How are paraphrasing and repeating different from each other?

Lesson 4

Objectives
Students will
- participate in a classic exercise that demonstrates "point of view";
- role-play situations in which characters have different points of view;
- Identify the problem and the feelings the characters are having;
- Coach the characters in solving the problems.

Materials
- Agenda on chart paper or the chalkboard
- Copies of Old Woman/Young Woman drawing for students (see handout at the end of the unit)

Gathering: Emotions in Music

Select several different types of musical pieces – for example, classical, hip-hop, jazz, reggae, blues, etc. Ask students to listen to a short segment from each piece with their full attention; they may want to close their eyes. At the end of each segment, ask students to describe the emotions they felt during that type of music. Use at least three different pieces of music that evoke different types of emotions. Students may have different responses to each piece. This is fine – use it as an opportunity to point out how we can have different perspectives about the same thing.

Check agenda

Go over the objectives and the agenda.

Point of View: The Young Woman and the Old Woman

One of the most interesting things about *Encounter* is the way it presents the different points of view of the Spanish and the Tainos. Since they came from such different cultures, the way they see things is dramatically different. The boy looks at the Spanish, sees that they cover their bodies and their feet, and concludes that they are not human beings. The Spanish look at the Tainos, who are scantily clad, and conclude that they are primitive. In both cases, the meaning they give to what they see is shaped by their previous experience. This is true to some extent for any two people, even when they come from the same culture, are roughly the same age, and have had many of the same kinds of experiences.

To illustrate this, we can use the classic exercise of the Young Woman/Old Woman drawing:

1. Make copies of the Young Woman/Old Woman drawing (see handout at the end of the unit) and distribute to the class.
2. Ask the students to work quietly on their own, studying the picture and writing a brief description of what they see in the picture.
3. Ask volunteers to share their descriptions with the class. Some students will see a young woman; others, an old woman. Let students who see the young woman explain how they see a young woman to those who see the old woman—and vice versa.
4. Discuss: Is there a "right" way to see the picture? Why do you think some saw an old woman and others a young woman? What conclusions do you come to from this exercise?

ROLE-PLAYS

In a conflict, each person has his or her own point of view, or way of seeing the situation. As the exercise of the Young Woman/Old Woman illustrates, two different people can take in exactly the same information—exactly the same behavior, words, gesture or series of events—and interpret it in different ways, find different meaning in it. We see this clearly in *Encounter*. In Book Talk, the class worked to understand the different points of view of the Tainos and the Spanish. In this activity, we further develop the children's understanding of "point of view." The teacher presents role-plays in which the characters come into conflict and have different points of view on the situation. The students try to understand where the characters are coming from and coach them about solutions to the problem.

Situation 1

The teacher plays a child, and a student volunteer plays the mother. Feel free to improvise on the script below.

Mother:	Clean up your room now.
Child:	I'm tired, Mom. I don't want to do it right now.
Mother:	It's like a pig pen. Dirty dishes, piles of dirty clothes on the floor. It'll attract roaches and germs. You'll get sick.
Child:	No, I won't, Mom. You're exaggerating. Anyway, I'll clean it. Just not now. I'm tired.
Mother:	There's always some excuse. Either you're tired or too busy. Meanwhile, the room gets messier and messier.
Child:	Mom, I wish you'd stop nagging me.

Pause the action. Ask, what is happening here? How do you think the characters are feeling? What's the point of view of the mother? The point of view of the child? Who do you think is right? Elicit the students' thinking. Point out that there isn't always a clear right or wrong in an argument. What do they agree with the mother about? What do they agree with the child about?

What advice would you give them for resolving their conflict?

Ask whether anyone has ever experienced a conflict like this? How did it turn out?

Situation 2

The teacher plays Ms./Mr. Brown, a teacher, and a student volunteer plays Joanna, a fifth grader. Feel free to improvise on the script.

Ms./Mr. Brown:	Joanna/John, may I speak to you for a moment?
Joanna/John:	Sure.
	[The two go to the teacher's desk to have a private conversation.]
Ms./Mr. Brown:	I've decided to change your seat so that you're not sitting next to Yvonne/Ivan.
Joanna/John:	Why? S/he's my best friend! We always sit together—ever since we've been in this school.
Ms./Mr. Brown:	I know. That's the problem. The two of you are always talking.
Joanna/John:	But all of the talking we do is about our work. You know that Yvonne/Ivan has trouble with reading and math. I'm helping her/him. She depends on me.
Ms./Mr. Brown:	I'm afraid s/he's depending on you too much. S/he counts on you for the answers, and that's keeping her/him from thinking for herself/himself. Also, I know you don't only talk about your work.
Joanna/John:	*[indignant]* I never give her/him the answers! I always ask questions! I make her/him think it out for herself. I'm a good teacher! Why don't you ask Yvonne/Ivan what s/he thinks? You can't split us up! We're best friends!
Ms./Mr. Brown:	I'm sorry, but I just don't think it's working.

Pause the action and this time, ask students to "Stop, Breathe and Think" (see Unit 2). Then guide the class in understanding the points of view of both characters, as you did above. Again, point out that in a conflict there's not always a clear-cut right or wrong. Where do you think the teacher might have a point? Where do you think Joanna/John might have a point? What advice would you give them for resolving their conflict so that both of them (and Yvonne/Ivan) feels good about it?

Situation 3

Get volunteers from the class to play two students, Michael and Jason (or Michele and Jasmine). Be sure the names are not those of anyone in the class.

M: Let's work at the computer.

J: No, I'd rather play with the Legos. We could build a city together.

M: Oh, come on. Legos are baby stuff. We could do some cool stuff with the computer. I'll show you.

J: Every time we have free time, we do what you want to do. This time I want to do what I want to do. Last time you promised that this time it would be my choice.

M: I know, but the computer is never open, and today it is. We finally have a chance to use it. I don't want to pass up the chance.

J: We agreed that this time it would be my choice.

Pause the action here, and guide the students in reflecting on the situation, as above.

Evaluation

What's one thing you liked about today's lesson? Give a few volunteers a chance to share their thoughts.

Closing: Applause

Lead the group in a round of applause.

Additional Activities

Who's missing?

The students are sitting in a circle in no particular order. A student leaves the room. While the student is gone, one or more students hides. The rest close in the circle. The returning student tries to figure out who's missing.

Changes

Part of good listening is being a keen observer. To sharpen students' powers of observation, introduce the game "Changes." The students work in pairs. The students turn back to back and one student changes three things about him- or herself while the other students stays with eyes closed. (The student might take off glasses, tuck in a shirt, untie shoes.) When they turn to face each other, the one who had eyes closed tries to identify the three changes. Then they switch.

Noticing Body Language

Throughout *Encounter*, the Taino and the strangers had to communicate through gestures and body language. Ask the class if they recall examples of this. Point out to them how much communication, particularly about emotions, happens through body language, rather than words.

As a way to become more aware of body language, show a short segment of a movie or TV show without any sound. Ask the class to note details of body language, and what they think is being communicated. What do you think each person in the film is feeling? How do you know?

Students may also do this as a homework assignment.

Discuss: How has body language given you clues into what another person is thinking or feeling? Have you ever misinterpreted someone's body language? Has anyone ever misinterpreted your body language? What can we do when this happens?

Create a Peace Corner in your classroom

Explain that you want the students' help in making a place in the classroom where they can go for a few minutes to relax if they are upset about something. <u>The Peace Corner will not be a place where a student is sent for a "time out." Going to the Peace Corner will be completely voluntary.</u> A good book for introducing students to the idea of a Peace Corner is *A Quiet Place* by Douglas Wood.

Have a space in mind that you and the class can turn into a little nook with a clear identity, distinct from the rest of the classroom. It should include a small table or desk and a blank wall above the desk that can be decorated with children's art. On the wall above the desk should be a beautiful sign, made by students, naming the space as the "Peace Corner."

Have the class brainstorm ideas of what might go into the Peace Corner: for example, paper and pencils for writing, crayons and paper for drawing, books about feelings, coloring books, a Hugg-A-Planet, a chart with the steps of Plan 1-2-3, photos of beautiful things from nature.

Involve the class in making ground rules for the use of the Peace Corner, for example,
- Ask the teacher's permission to go to the Peace Corner
- Return to your regular classroom activities as soon as you feel ready
- Take yourself to a peaceful place in your mind
- Use Plan 1-2-3 to cool yourself down

With the students' help, set up the Peace Corner and see how it goes!

Set aside time for silence and breathing

The school day is hectic and stressful for students and teachers. It's useful to build in time each day for a few minutes of silence. During this time the lights are off. No writing, drawing, reading. Just sitting. Students can close their eyes if they want. You can tell them that they can let their minds use the silence as they wish. Or you can suggest ways they might use the silence. For example, to

- practice abdominal breathing.
- pay attention to their breathing
- pay attention to sounds they hear

- take themselves to a peaceful place in their mind
- recall a time they had fun
- recall something they like to do

Be sure to take this opportunity to enjoy a couple of minutes of silence yourself.

Make "time for silence" part of your daily routine. You might carve out a few minutes for silence when the students come back from lunch and recess, or at the beginning or end of the day as well as after lunch.

A few minutes of silence at strategic times during the day will pay off in a calmer, more focused class. And you'll be developing in your students a habit and skill that will serve them well throughout their lives.

Consider having your students keep a 4Rs journal

Writing (drawing for younger students) is an excellent way to reinforce and consolidate learning. A journal enables students to put all of their Book Talk writing in one place. You can also give them a few minutes after each 4Rs lesson to jot down a few thoughts about what they're taking away or how they're planning to use what they've just learned. If a student tries a new skill, s/he might want to write about what happened. Did it bring a positive result? If a student is stuck in a conflict with someone, s/he might want to do some writing to sort it out and imagine some solutions. You can give them standard journals and encourage them to decorate them.

By having students keep journals, you will be introducing them to a habit or practice that can serve them well the rest of their lives.

Related Books

The Bat-Poet by Randall Jarrell, illustrated by Maurice Sendak
Christopher Columbus by Jan Gleiter, illustrated by Kathleen Thompson
Columbus and the Renaissance Explorers by Colin Hynson
Columbus: The Triumphant Failure by Oliver Postgate, illustrated by Naomi Linnel
The Discovery of the Americas by Betsy and Giulio Maestro
From Slave Ship to Freedom Road by Julius Lester, illustrated by Rod Brown
If You Were There in 1492 by Barbara Brenner
Rethinking Columbus: The Next 500 Years by Bill Bigelow, Bob Peterson, ed. (resources for teachers, including material on Thanksgiving, has a role-play putting Columbus on trial)
Shades of Gray by Carolyn Reeder
The Truth about Columbus by James W. Loewen (posters and resource material for teachers)
Walk Two Moons by Sharon Creech

Young Woman / Old Woman

Picture designed by the American psychologist E.G. Boring

5

Unit 4 Theme

Learning to Be Assertive

Unit 4 Book Selection

Your Move by Eve Bunting. Harcourt Brace, 1998

Activities

- Choices
- Strong, Mean, and Giving In
- Consequences
- I-Messages
- Draining
- Assertiveness Line
- Additional Activities

Introduction

Assertive behavior helps us to pursue our needs and protect our space and interests without dominating or abusing others. We can look at assertiveness in the following schema:

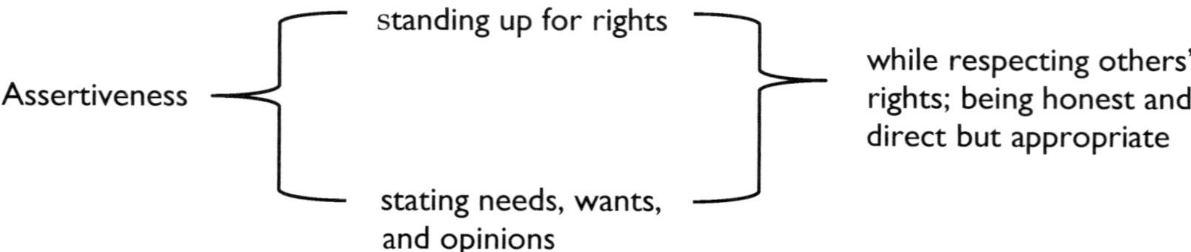

Children see few models of assertive behavior. Too many adults use their unequal power to threaten children. Television, video, and movie characters often act aggressively or respond to aggression with hostile acts. More and more, we see adults and children who can only respond to threats (real or imagined) with violence.

Being assertive is a stance toward life. The assertive person is neither victim nor bully. Assertiveness, like active listening, involves a set of skills that can be learned. Students will find assertiveness skills useful in such situations as

- dealing with teasing and bullying
- dealing with peer pressure, saying no to things they don't want to do and putting forth their point of view even when it's not the popular thing to say
- handling issues with friends and family
- asking for what they need
- standing up to injustice

True strength comes from self-knowledge. We can learn how to know ourselves better through reading, reflecting, and writing—How is this character feeling? What do you think the character will do? Have you ever felt this way? What would you do? Using this knowledge, we will be better prepared to make wise choices. We can practice assertiveness skills through group discussions, role-plays, and paired exercises.

In this curriculum, we explore the factors that allow students to develop assertive behavior and present techniques for developing such behavior. In the lower grades, we focus on the basics: saying no and stating needs clearly. In the upper grades, we add additional strategies, such as I-messages, which are useful with people who care about our feelings.

In this unit

	Ideas	Skills
Literacy	We can see clues in a story as to what will happen next (foreshadowing) Stories can be told by one of the characters in the story (first-person narrative) Conflicts in stories can be inside a character or between characters	• Identifying the main idea • Asking questions • Expressing ideas clearly Providing evidence to back up one's assertions • Predicting the outcome • Describing scenes
Social and Emotional Learning	• Anticipating consequences • Making choices • Being assertive	Identifying options in a conflict situation • Predicting consequences • "Strong" assertive behavior • I-Messages

Your Move, by Eve Bunting, illus. by James Ransome. Harcourt Brace, 1998.

SUMMARY

Ten-year-old James and his six-year-old brother, Isaac, have to stay alone in the evenings while their mother goes to work. James knows that his brother looks up to him ("Now that Dad's gone he thinks I'm smarter than anybody.") and copies his every move. Usually the boys do homework, play games, or watch television. But tonight is going to be different. They are sneaking out to take part in an initiation rite to a "club" that James wants to be part of, the K-Bones. Every hour the boys have to thump on their neighbors' wall so that she knows they're all right. They plan to do what they need to do and be back in an hour. As they start out, James is slightly apprehensive. He wants to be part of the club, which he keeps telling himself is just that, not a crew, or gang. We meet the boys in the K-Bones, a group put together by the leaders Kris and Bones. Kris holds up a can of spray paint and tells James that he's going to do some writing. James calls it by its name: tagging. "'Crews tag, we write,'" Bones says. He throws a punch at Isaac to include him in the group. Isaac is excited to be with the older guys. James gets even more nervous when he finds out that the writing will be on a traffic sign above the thruway. He holds Isaac's hand crossing the street, but Isaac tries to pull away. The author describes the path to the sign and we share James's increasing nervousness. When Isaac realizes how high the sign is, he tries to dissuade James. James wants to "slink away," but he must prove himself. He climbs a pole that is vibrating from the heavy traffic and stands on an electrical box in order to reach out and spray the words "K-Bones" over the name of a gang called the Snakes. When he is back on the ground again, he savors the feeling of being "so cool." Still, he can't enjoy if for long, because Kris is afraid that someone may have reported them to the police, so they start running. As they run, James asks Kris if this is a common activity. "'Sometimes we play the "take-it" game. You know, take it from the minimarket, take it from Bates Drugs.'" "'You mean steal?'" "'No, it's a game.'" Kris insists. James is having second thoughts. "I should have known the kind of stuff the K-Bones do. I'm not that dumb. Maybe I did know. But I wanted to be in with them."

Suddenly they run into the Snakes, older boys who, James realizes, will go "right back up that pole and write over what I just wrote." He can see the endless escalation in front of him, when Bones shouts that they should run "'They've got a gun!'" They flee. He hears a shot, and when his brother falls, he thinks Isaac has been shot. But "'it's just that I'm pulling him too fast.'" Isaac screams at him to stop. After checking to be sure that the Snakes are not in pursuit, James tends to his brother. Isaac's jeans are torn and his knees are bloody. Then "he really starts screaming."

When the boys arrive home they find their mother and next-door neighbor, Mrs. Lopez. She had alerted their mother when she didn't hear the thump after an hour. "'I have to be able to trust you, James,'" his mother says. But she no longer does, and she tells them that she will somehow find the money for a sitter to watch them. In the meantime, they have to thump on the wall ever half hour.

The next night, Kris arrives. He sees Isaac's bandages and asks how he is. "'He could have been dead,'" James retorts, but Kris dismisses his anger and says that soon the K-Bones, too, will have a gun. He is happy to announce that not only has James been elected to the club, so has Isaac, even "'though you're just a little punk.'" He hands James a Lakers cap, the new club emblem, which James is sure has been stolen. "'Thanks, but no thanks,'" says James. Kris turns to Isaac and hands him a "brand, sparkling new, purple and gold" cap. "He wants this cap, I can tell," James thinks. Isaac sighs, "'Thanks, but no thanks.'" Kris is "really mad. When he slams the door behind him the whole apartment shakes."

The boys return to their checkerboard. James makes a move. Isaac copies him. "'You're so weird, Isaac,' I say. But it's OK. He's only six. And I'm his brother."

COMMENT

Vivid descriptions and tense scenes draw the reader into this classic story of a young person who wants to belong to a group whose norms are in conflict with parental values. James knows better, but his desire to be cool overcomes both his sense of responsibility and common sense. There is the story of Isaac, the younger brother who trusts James and who could be injured or morally stunted by James's choices. We see him at the beginning of the adventure wanting to be as "grown-up" as the others. There is their mother, probably working two jobs, although we are not told this; struggling to provide for the family, but perhaps putting too much responsibility on the shoulders of a ten-year-old. There is Mrs. Lopez, part of their community, who makes it possible for their mother to enforce her rules. We see here some of the building blocks of conflict resolution: community, an ability to articulate feelings, listening for what is really being said ("'You mean stealing?'", and finally the ability to be assertive in the face of anger and ridicule. James proves himself to the "club," but he is aware of his own feelings and the moral precepts of his community to know that he would be making the wrong choice to go with the K-Bones. We can almost see the progression that members of the Snakes may have taken, from eager tag-alongs to proud rule-breakers to menacing young adults. The baby punks on page 7 could easily become the scowling gang members on page 20.

We see how the author uses foreshadowing to emphasize the impact on Isaac's life of James's choices. We can look at the use of slang in writing and talk about whether it helps or hinders the narrative. We can explore the symbolism of the word "move, "the use of euphemisms in people's lives ("'Crews tag, we write.'"). We can talk about peer pressure, the influence of family on our choices, options beyond "Thanks, but no thanks," the meaning of courage, and the extra pressure on children who have to grow up fast because the adults in their lives are missing or unable to be with them.

Book Talk

READ-ALOUD

Previewing the book

Show the cover and ask what students think the book will be about. What kinds of moves do people make? Read the dedications in the back. (Diane D'Andrade is an author and has been the editor for many of Eve Bunting's books. Biggie Smalls was a rapper who was gunned down in his early twenties, presumably because of rival gang warfare.) Tholes means to endure. Ask the students to be alert for clues about where the action of the book takes place. If you're sure your class is aware of the slang in the book, don't dwell on it, but if it's unfamiliar, review it (tag, crew).

Reading and responding to the book

Read the book through without stopping.

After you read the story, ask the students to pair up and talk about the story. What interests them? What questions do they have?   Ask students to share their questions and comments with the class. Ask what was important to them about each story. Encourage as much class participation as possible by asking questions. If others want to respond to a comment from one student, suggest that they restate in their own words what the child has said, then give their opinion and their reasons.

Deepening students' understanding of the book

Ask students what they think this book is about. Get as many ideas as you can. It is an adventure, it is a morality tale, it is a coming-of-age story. We want to look at the ways in which James grows throughout the book, from being a person who somewhat reluctantly cares for his younger brother and craves the respect of older kids and the sense of security of belonging to a group to being someone who recognizes his responsibility to his sibling and is able to listen to his own voice rather than the voices of those in the club. As he grows into his responsibility and awareness, he acts assertively.

Make a chart of the main characters and ask students what each character was probably feeling at various points in the story. (Mom, James, Isaac, Mrs. Lopez, Kris). Ask them to support their ideas with examples from the text.

Make a list of the slang words in the text. If students know different slang for the same word, write it in parentheses next to it. Why do we think the author used slang? What does the use of slang add to the story? Does it take anything away from the story?

List the conflicts in the book (James in self-conflict, K-Bones in conflict with Snakes, James and Isaac in conflict with Kris). How are the conflicts different? Similar?

What is James looking for by joining the K-Bones? Ask the students to make a T-chart, writing advantages in one column and disadvantages in the other column. Then make a class chart. Ask students for reasons that James might have wanted to join (excitement, a sense of belonging, adventure, challenge, a chance to prove himself as a young man, being cool). What are the things he found out about the club that went against his values or that he thought were stupid and dangerous (getting a gun, competition with the Snakes, stealing, major risk-taking)? The things he wants are not necessarily bad. It's just that they come mixed in with other things that he sees will not be good for him *or* Isaac. What do we know about James's life and his character that help us understand why he made the choices he did?

Have students draw a courage web and ask them to give examples of all the ways that James shows courage, then discuss different types of courage (climbing the pole to spray paint, staying with his brother as they run from the gun shots even though it slows him down, standing up to Kris, staying home alone with his brother). Then draw a class web. Discuss different types of courage. What enabled James to resist peer pressure and stand up to Kris?

Connecting the book to students' lives

Discussion: Have students had the experience of wanting to be part of a group that their parents or guardians didn't approve of? What was good about wanting it or belonging to it and what wasn't so great?

Does anyone know someone who is in a gang or a clique? Do they know people who could be in gangs or cliques but aren't? Do they know how those people stayed out? What assertive strategies did they use? Do they think that everyone who is not part of such a group secretly wants to be "in"?

Point out this passage on p. 5: "Kris rattles a can of spray paint. 'Just some writing,' he says. I take a deep breath. 'You mean tagging?'" Remind students about how they have used abdominal breathing in the 4Rs, and the role of breathing in Plan 1-2-3. Why did James take the deep breath before asking Kris about tagging?

What are the sources of James's strength? What are sources of strength for you?

Writing: Ask students to write about a time when they did something they thought was dangerous or off-putting but that they were proud of doing. It doesn't have to be reckless; it could be crossing the street for the first time when they were little or riding a roller coaster or touching a particularly slimy creature.

Ask students to write about a time when their actions and their thoughts didn't match. For example, as James approached the highway sign, he was secretly wishing that Isaac could pull him away, but he went ahead with climbing up to the sign anyway. His thoughts and feelings were telling him one thing, but his actions were the opposite. What is it like to be in a situation like this?

The class could make a dictionary of slang in use at your school.

Ask the students to write a scene where they say yes to a group they want to belong to.
Then ask them to write a scene in which they say no.

ROLE-PLAY

James's brother, Isaac, is telling a friend in school about the evening's adventures and how it
all turned out. The listener can practice the Three Ps of active listening.

Applied Learning

SOCIAL AND EMOTIOAL LEARNING LESSONS

Introductory note to the teacher

Students meet situations every day in which they must decide how to balance their own
interests in relation to the interests of other people:

- You want to be alone, but a friend wants to be with you. What do you do?
- A classmate teases you or calls you a name. How do you respond?
- You're walking along a busy city street with your mom and decide you want an ice
  cream cone. You know your mom won't be enthusiastic about the idea. How do you
  ask?
- Your family is having a conversation around the dinner table, and you have an opinion
  you'd like to state, but everyone is talking so fast. How do you get people to listen to
  what <u>you</u> have to say?
- An older kid says you have to give him the cake from your lunch or he'll beat you up.
- Two close friends ask you to join them in stealing money from another kid's backpack.
- Your younger brother keeps bothering you when you're trying to do your homework.

In these situations, children need to know that they have choices. They can go on the attack.
They can stand up for their interests or convictions. Or they can give in, going along with
the other person's request, even though they don't want to. Adults call these choices
"aggression," "assertiveness," and "submission." With children, we speak of being mean,
being strong, and giving in.

It's not easy for youngsters to resist the pull of their peers, as *Your Move* demonstrates.
There's excitement in hanging with the K-Bones and a sense of belonging. There's also
danger, and James is forced to make a hard choice. Ultimately he sees his situation clearly,
and decides to stand up for what is right. Predictably, Kris is not pleased and James has to

endure his displeasure. The story underlines the importance of helping students develop skills in saying no and standing firm.

Although in this guide we're partial to assertiveness, there is no one right way to respond to the myriad of complex situations children (or adults) confront daily. Sometimes we'll agree to "give in" and let a friend join us even if we really want to be alone. We may see that the friend is feeling blue and needs some companionship; or perhaps the friend has a compelling reason for spending time with us now — she's going away or has something important to tell us. Sometimes we may need to be very firm to get our point across to someone who just "isn't getting it," and that person may experience us as mean.

Our aim is that children learn to think flexibly in order to come up with the approach that fits the situation and develop skills to carry it out. This means showing youngsters that they have a range of choices in any given situation and expanding their repertoire of ways to be strong. Too often children (and adults) in our society fall into the habit of being aggressive or submissive rather than taking the path that is usually most effective in the long run: assertiveness.

Like active listening, assertiveness is a stance toward life, a way of being in the world. Like active listening, assertiveness also involves a set of skills we can practice and improve. With young children (grades K-2)) we focus on the most basic skills of assertiveness: saying no; and making a strong, clear, confident statement of what you want. With older children, we introduce additional strategies, such as "I-messages."

In Book Talk, we sought to understand the characters (James, his mother, Isaac)--their sources of strength, the reasons they made the decisions they did. Here in the Applied Learning Section, we apply ideas of assertiveness to other kinds of situations our students face daily and give them a chance to practice skills in standing up for themselves and being strong.

Lesson 1

Objectives

Students will
- observe a role-play in which two friends are having a conflict;
- describe the problem and how the characters are feeling;
- identify the choices the characters have in the situation.

Materials

- Agenda on chart paper or the chalkboard

Gathering: Where's Your Mind?

Ask students to practice a minute or two of abdominal breathing.

Ring a chime, and ask the students to go around the circle and describe a thought or feeling they had while doing abdominal breathing by completing this sentence: "Right now, my mind is on…" Any response is fine: "what I had for breakfast," "the math test coming up," "vacation," "my sore knee," "what my mother said to me this morning," etc.

Point out that we all have thoughts and feelings going on in our minds that others may not realize. Ask for a show of hands about how many thoughts or feelings were about something in the past, how many were about something in the future, and how many were about the present.

Check agenda

Go over the objectives and the agenda.

Choices

Role-plays are useful for working on assertiveness with students in Grades 3-5. The role-play below picks up on the theme of being different as well as on the challenge of standing up to peer pressure. If it doesn't seem appropriate for your class, please create another tailored to your class's needs or use one of the many other possible role-plays described below (see "Other Situations")

Here's the situation. Jennie is different from the other kids in the class in several ways: she always wears dresses (rather than the jeans and T-shirts the other kids wear); the dresses often seem out of style and a bit big on her; she's shy; and whether in the classroom, the lunchroom, or the school yard, she always carries a notebook around with her for her favorite activity, writing.

Victoria is the most popular girl in the class, a leader. She decides she wants to have some fun by getting several other girls to join her in a plan to get Jennie's notebook away from her and hide it.

Victoria approaches Latoya, one of several girls in the class who like to hang out with her, and tells her of the plan. "The only time she isn't holding that stupid notebook is when she works at the computer," says Victoria. "Watch her closely and when you get your chance, take the notebook and give it to me. I'll find a good place for it."

Latoya admires Victoria and enjoys being her friend. Being friends with Victoria gives her status in the class. However, she doesn't like this idea. First, she's pretty sure that if she takes part in the scheme, she'll get in trouble. But she also has nothing against Jennie. Sure, she's a little strange, but Jennie has always been nice to her; in fact, Jennie gave her half of her sandwich when she'd forgotten her lunch one day.

So Latoya doesn't want to take part in Victoria's plan. In fact, she doesn't want Victoria to do anything to hurt Jennie. But it's also important for her to remain Victoria's friend. And she doesn't want the other kids in the class to look down on her, as they do Jennie.

Ask for three volunteers: one to play Victoria, one to play Latoya, and one to be the narrator (who will fill in necessary background). Brief your actors on their roles. Make nametags for them with the names they will have in the role-play. Use the names suggested above only if they are not the names of any students in your class. (You can also change the names and situation to fit boys.)

A good ritual for beginning role-plays is to lead the class saying in unison, "Lights, camera, action!"

Run the skit.

Freeze the action while Victoria is still trying to convince Latoya to help her carry out her plan.

Explain that this would be a good time for Latoya to use Plan 1-2-3 (STOP, BREATHE, THINK). You'll help the students use Plan 1-2-3 to help them think about the right choice for Latoya to make. Lead the students in doing three cycles of abdominal breathing as introduced in Unit 2.

After the breathing, ask, what is happening? Encourage the students to describe what is going on as objectively as possible. Then ask, how do you think the characters are feeling?

Ask, what are Latoya's <u>choices</u>? What are the different ways she might deal with the situation?

Elicit the students' ideas and chart them. Push them to come up with a wide range of possibilities.

Discuss: What do you think is the right thing for Latoya to do in this situation? Why? Do you think that will be easy or hard for her? What would you do? Why?

Evaluation

What was your favorite activity in this lesson?

Closing: Applause

Lead the students in a round of applause.

Lesson 2

Objectives

Students will
- learn the words "strong," "mean," and "giving in" to describe the choices they have in conflict situations;
- apply those ideas to clarify the choices faced by characters in a role-play;
- practice predicting the results or consequences of certain choices.

Materials

- Agenda on chart paper or the chalkboard

Gathering: Freeze

Play a piece of music and ask students to move around the room in any way they like, while respecting others' personal space. Tell the students that when the music stops, they should "freeze" as if they were a statue. They can only move when the music starts again. While "frozen," they can take a moment to notice each other's statues. Repeat several times, varying the amount of time that the music plays. This develops listening skills and the ability to physically self-monitor and self-regulate.

Check agenda

Go over the objectives and the agenda.

Strong, mean, and giving in (assertive, aggressive, submissive)

Introduce the words "strong," "mean," and "giving in." The students will probably have a good idea of the usual meanings of these words. Elicit their understandings. Then summarize the discussion by putting forth the following definitions:

- **Strong** = being nice and respecting the other person while standing up firmly for yourself (your rights, your interests);

- **Mean** = doing something to hurt another person (their body or their feelings) or using force or threats to make somebody do something they don't want to do; and

- **Giving in** = going along with what someone wants you to do even though you'd rather do something else.

For each of the three definitions, elicit examples from the students. (Depending on the age and maturity of your students, you may also want to introduce them to the "adult" words: assertive, aggressive, and submissive.)

Now apply those categories of response to the choices Latoya had in her interaction with Victoria. Which were "giving in"? Which were "strong"? Were any "mean"?

Consequences

Refer to the role-play with Victoria and Latoya. Ask the students to recall the situation. Say that one way to make a good choice is to think ahead about what is likely to happen as a result of your choice.

Select student volunteers to replay the skit as before, except this time they will act out one of the ideas the class proposed as choices for Latoya. Confer with the student playing Latoya and ask her to decide which course of action she'll have Latoya follow. It can be any of the choices; it doesn't have to be the one the student thinks is best.

Run the skit: "Lights, camera, action!"

Freeze the action after the two characters have had some dialogue back and forth. Ask the students to describe what has happened in the role-play. What choice did the character Latoya make? How has Victoria responded? What do they think will happen next?

Have student actors act out several of Latoya's choices and discuss as above. The aim is not to arrive at a definitive answer about what will happen in any given situation, but to show the children that it's possible—and important—to anticipate consequences.

Evaluation

What's one thing you want to remember from our lesson today?

Closing: Something I'm looking forward to

Give the students a minute or two to talk with a partner about something they're looking forward to today or in the next few days. Then ask a couple of volunteers to share with the group.

Lesson 3

Objective

- Students will learn "I-messages" as one technique for assertive or "strong" behavior.

Materials

- Agenda on chart paper or the chalkboard
- Hugg-A-Planet or other soft object
- Copies of I-message worksheet (see handout at the end of the unit)

Gathering: Freeze 2

Repeat the "Freeze" activity from Unit 4, Lesson 2. This time, when you stop the music, call out either "strong," "mean," or "giving in." Students must make a statue that expresses their understanding of these terms.

After a few minutes, ask students to say what they noticed about the statues for each term. How were they different? How did each posture feel?

Check agenda

Go over the objectives and the agenda.

I-messages

So far we've been helping students with two kinds of assertiveness skills: saying no and stating clearly and confidently what they want or what they believe to be right. Here we introduce a strategy that is sometimes useful in dealing with problems that come up with friends and family, that is, people who are likely to care about our feelings.

Begin by writing "I-message" on the board. Explain that today the students will learn what an I-message is and how to construct one.

An "I-message" is a way to be strong without being mean when you are angry or upset or disappointed (or whatever) with something another person has done. The formula for an "I-message" is as follows:

I feel ____
              (state your feeling)

when you ____
               (describe the specific behavior)

because ____
              (state the effect the behavior has on you)

The "I-message" is different from a "You-message." In a "You-message," you attack the other person, make judgments about the person, sometimes even call the person names.

For example, say your younger brother borrows your bat and leaves it at a friend's house. A "You-message" would be: "You jerk. How could you be so stupid! Now I don't have my bat when I need it!"

In this situation, what would an "I-message" be? Elicit possible "I-messages" from the students (for example: I feel frustrated when you borrow my bat and leave it at your friend's house, because I need it today and it's not here).

Discuss: What are your comments about these two ways of communicating feelings? Can you see using an "I-message" the next time you feel like calling somebody a name? Why? Why not?

Have students work in pairs to complete the worksheet on "I-messages" (see handout at the end of the unit). You can use the "Assertiveness line" (introduced in Lesson 4 of this unit) and "Strong Message Machine" (see Additional Activities in this unit) to give them more practice.

Draining*

Invite students to stand, and think of a situation in which they felt angry or fearful. Ask them to tense their muscles and hold tightly for a few seconds. Then tell them to relax, and feel the emotion draining out of them into a puddle at their feet. Then, have them step aside, leaving the feeling behind.

Ask students what this was like. When could you use this? They may make connections to the idea that using "strong" messages and I-messages is easier when we have recognized and released some of our anger or fear. Note that in *Your Move*, James had to confront and manage his conflicting emotions in order to finally use assertive behavior with Kris.

Adapted from *Creative Conflict Resolution* by William Kreidler, p. 120.

Evaluation and Closing: Connections

Set a timer for three minutes. Explain that this is a time to pause and think back over today's lesson or anything else that has happened today that's on your mind. Nobody has to say anything, but anyone who wants to say something to the group can raise their hand, you'll give them the Hugg-A-Planet or talking piece, and they can talk. People can share something they learned, something they're thinking about, a feeling they're having, whatever. Tell them to keep their comments brief so that others can talk. When the time runs out, "Connections" is over.

Lesson 4

Objectives

Students will
- practice "strong" (assertive) behavior in role-plays;
- continue to deepen their understanding of "strong," "mean," and "giving in" by discussing which of the categories applies to specific examples.

Materials

- Agenda on chart paper or chalkboard

Gathering: Going to middle school

Next year, the students in the class will be going to middle school. Ask students to pair up and discuss the following: What's one thing you're looking forward to about that and one thing you're not looking forward to?

After a couple of minutes of talking in pairs, give several volunteers a chance to share with the group.

Check agenda

Go over the objectives and the agenda.

Assertiveness line

Role-plays in front of the class are useful for introducing ideas such as choice, consequences, and assertiveness. But only a few students are actively participating while most of the class observes. Other kinds of activities are necessary to give the students practice.

In an "assertiveness line," the students form two lines with students in Line A facing students in Line B so that each student has a partner.

You can say, "All the students in this line are Student A and all the students in this line are Student B. A was using a marker and put it down for a minute to ask the teacher a question. B took the marker and is now using it. A wants the marker back. Does everybody understand the situation? Okay. When I say 'Go,' begin acting out the situation. When I say 'Freeze,' stop immediately and get quiet. No touching the other person." [You may want to practice the freeze command with the students several times to show them that you expect them to stop immediately and be completely quiet.]

Say "Go!" Let the action run for a minute or so. Stop the action. Ask, what happened in your pairs? How did Student A try to get the marker back? What did Student B do? As volunteers share what happened in their pair, ask what kind of response they used? Strong? Mean? Giving in? After hearing from several pairs, say that when you say Go, you want them to do the skit again. This time you want Student A in all of the pairs to try a strong response.

Continue with other situations. Make up ones relevant to your class or use the suggestions included in this unit under "Additional Activities." With later scenarios, consider asking students to use Plan 1-2-3, "Stop-Breathe-Think" (introduced in Unit 2) when the action is stopped. Ask: How does this affect how the scenario plays out? Can using Plan 1-2-3 help us better use assertiveness? Why or why not?

Evaluation

Was it easy or hard to think of "strong" things to do in your assertiveness line? Can you see yourself acting that way in real life? Why? Why not?

Closing: Pass the sound

Play "Pass the Sound" as in Unit 1, Lesson 2. Begin by making a sound. "Pass" the sound to a student. Ask the student to imitate the sound you are making and then change it into another sound. S/he passes it to another person who repeats the new sound and changes it again. Continue around the group.

Additional Activities

Other situations

Invent other skits that present situations students encounter daily. Choose situations that your particular class is confronting and struggling with. Use the skits to deepen their awareness of choices and consequences and to increase their repertoire of "strong" responses. Here's a list of the kinds of situations in which students may find "strong" or assertive behavior helpful:

- expressing needs or desires clearly and firmly without whining
- dealing with teasing
- dealing with bullying
- dealing with peer pressure
- dealing with problems with friends (hurt feelings, misunderstandings, broken promises, etc.)
- dealing with things that don't seem fair

Here are some possible scenarios for skits:

- Yvonne is teasing Jessica . [You supply the specific pretext for the teasing based on the kinds of things that come up in your class. But avoid choosing a scenario that directly calls attention to a specific instance of teasing and therefore might add to the hurt of the child who was teased. Do not use an example for which "Jessica" could actually be teased.] Ask the class to imagine themselves as a third person seeing this. Yvonne is a leader in the class. Jessica is not popular but she's always been nice to you. You as a third party want to stop the teasing. What can you do?

- The same skit as above (between Yvonne and Jessica), but this time, no one else is around. What can Jessica do?

- John approaches his best friend, Sean, and offers him a candy bar. "Where did you get it?" Sean asks. "From Joan's backpack," whispers John. "No one saw me take it." Sean is afraid of getting in trouble if he takes the stolen candy. He also knows that he wouldn't like it if someone stole from his backpack. He doesn't want to take the candy bar. What does he say to John?

- Betty and Naomi are good friends. They agree that tomorrow they'll dress exactly the same—all in black. They agree that if for some reason one person can't do this, then that person will be sure to text the other to let her know. Betty comes to school dressed in black, but Naomi comes in blue jeans and a red shirt. Betty is furious. What does she do?

- You're playing football in the schoolyard during recess with a group of boys. The sides are uneven: four on one side, three on the other. A girl comes up and says she wants to play. One of the boys immediately says, "No. You can't play. No girls allowed!" You know this isn't right and want to stand up for the girl. What do you do?

Strong message machine

This is another activity that gives students the opportunity for practice. Have them form two lines facing each other as for the "assertiveness line" above. But this time, they are a "strong message machine." Present a situation. Two kids are teasing another student because they say s/he talks funny. "You can't talk!" They chant. "You can't talk!" The student has just come from another country and doesn't know much English. You want to stop the teasing. What do you do?

Ask the students to talk with their partners (that is, the student facing them in the line) and think of a strong message to give the teasers to make them stop. Give them a minute to come up with something.

Then the teacher walks between the two lines. S/he stops at a student and pretends to "turn the machine on" (by pressing an imaginary button or turning a knob). That student says a strong message. The teacher says "Thank you," and then walks further down between the lines, stopping to turn another imaginary knob and hear a strong message from that student. And so on.

After you're done with the machine, discuss: What were your favorite "strong" messages? Why did you like them?

Create a Peace Corner in your classroom

Explain that you want the students' help in making a place in the classroom where they can go for a few minutes to relax if they are upset about something. <u>The Peace Corner will not be a place where a student is sent for a "time out." Going to the Peace Corner will be completely voluntary.</u> A good book for introducing students to the idea of a Peace Corner is *A Quiet Place* by Douglas Wood.

Have a space in mind that you and the class can turn into a little nook with a clear identity, distinct from the rest of the classroom. It should include a small table or desk and a blank wall above the desk that can be decorated with children's art. On the wall above the desk should be a beautiful sign, made by students, naming the space as the "Peace Corner."

Have the class brainstorm ideas of what might go into the Peace Corner: for example, paper and pencils for writing, crayons and paper for drawing, books about feelings, coloring books, a Hugg-A-Planet, a chart with the steps of Plan 1-2-3, photos of beautiful things from nature.

Involve the class in making ground rules for the use of the Peace Corner, for example,
- Ask the teacher's permission to go to the Peace Corner
- Return to your regular classroom activities as soon as you feel ready
- Take yourself to a peaceful place in your mind
- Use Plan 1-2-3 to cool yourself down

With the students' help, set up the Peace Corner and see how it goes!

Set aside time for silence and breathing

The school day is hectic and stressful for students and teachers. It's useful to build in time each day for a few minutes of silence. During this time the lights are off. No writing, drawing, reading. Just sitting. Students can close their eyes if they want. You can tell them that they can let their minds use the silence as they wish. Or you can suggest ways they might use the silence. For example, to

- practice abdominal breathing.
- pay attention to their breathing
- pay attention to sounds they hear
- take themselves to a peaceful place in their mind
- recall a time they had fun
- recall something they like to do

Be sure to take this opportunity to enjoy a couple of minutes of silence yourself.

Make "time for silence" part of your daily routine. You might carve out a few minutes for silence when the students come back from lunch and recess, or at the beginning or end of the day as well as after lunch.

A few minutes of silence at strategic times during the day will pay off in a calmer, more focused class. And you'll be developing in your students a habit and skill that will serve them well throughout their lives.

Consider having your students keep a 4Rs journal

Writing (drawing for younger students) is an excellent way to reinforce and consolidate learning. A journal enables students to put all of their Book Talk writing in one place. You can also give them a few minutes after each 4Rs lesson to jot down a few thoughts about what they're taking away or how they're planning to use what they've just learned. If a student tries a new skill, s/he might want to write about what happened. Did it bring a positive result? If a student is stuck in a conflict with someone, s/he might want to do some writing to sort it out and imagine some solutions. You can give them standard journals and encourage them to decorate them.

By having students keep journals, you will be introducing them to a habit or practice that can serve them well the rest of their lives.

Related Books

Jumping the Nail by Eve Bunting

On My Honor by Marion Dane Bauer

Stay True: Stories for Strong Girls compiled by Marilyn Singer

Design an I-message
for each of the following situations:

1. You lent your new bike to a friend. When s/he returns it, it has a flat tire. You decide to give your friend an I-message.

    I feel ____

    when you ____

    because ____

2. Your older brother or sister promised to take you to the movies. You've been really looking forward to it. At the last minute s/he says something has come up and s/he won't be able to do it. You decide to give your brother/ sister an I-message.

    I feel ____

    when you ____

    because ____

3. You and your younger brother/sister share a room at home. When it comes to tidying up the room, you feel you're the one who ends up doing all the work. You decide to give your brother/sister an I-message.

    I feel ____

    when you ____

    because ____

4. When you get home from school, you go to the kitchen to get a piece of pie. It turns out that your sister just ate the last two pieces.

    I feel ____

    when you ____

    because ____

5

Unit 5 Theme

Solving Problems Collaboratively

Unit 5 Book Selection

Brothers in Hope: The Story of the Lost Boys of Sudan
by Mary Williams, illustrated by R. Gregory Christie
Lee and Low Books Inc., 2005

Activities

- Defining "Conflict"
- Web: What's Good about Conflict?
- Win-Win Solutions
- Positions vs. Needs
- Defining Negotiation
- Introduction to Win-Win Negotiation
- Practicing Win-Win Negotiation
- Problem-Solving: ABCDE Approach
- De-escalating Conflict
- Introduction to Mediation (optional)
- Additional Activities

Introduction

Conflict. The word can make our stomachs tense or send adrenaline rushing through our bodies. Most people have a flight or fight reaction to conflict, and most people don't think of conflict as a constructive force. In this unit we will look at conflict both as a process to be managed or resolved without flight or a violent fight and as a force that in some cases can deepen our self-knowledge and lead to closeness and personal growth. We will look at varieties of conflicts, especially those in school, and varieties of responses. We will sharpen our ability to deal well with conflict by applying skills from previous units and practicing some new skills, such as win-win negotiation. Although it is not possible for every conflict to be solved to the satisfaction of all parties, our emphasis will be on learning to reach win-win solutions.

Conflict is a natural part of life. We encounter conflict every day. Some conflicts are inevitable (clashes over opposing needs, goals, or values), and some are unnecessary or avoidable (results of misunderstandings, ignorance, prejudice, poor organizational structure, poor communication, etc.). Conflicts bring up feelings, which is perfectly natural. Although we often think that conflict must lead to violence, it doesn't have to, especially if we have skills in conflict resolution.

Robert Bolton, in *People Skills*, identifies three kinds of conflicts: conflicts of emotion, of values, and of need. Active listening is key in dealing with conflicts of emotion. Value conflicts can seldom be resolved, but conflict resolution skills can help the parties understand each other better and show greater tolerance. Conflicts of need can often be resolved through the methods covered in this unit: negotiation, mediation, and problem solving. Ironically, the avoidable conflicts rooted in misunderstanding and prejudice may be less amenable to these methods and may best be dealt with through assertiveness.

> **Negotiation** is a process by which two or more parties talk together in order to arrive at an agreement. We all negotiate every day.
>
> ______________
>
> **Mediation** is a process in which a neutral facilitator helps parties to a dispute talk out their differences. The decision-making power stays in the hands of the disputants.
>
> ______________
>
> **Arbitration** is a process in which disputants present their points of view to a judge or arbitrator, who hands down a decision.

In this unit

	Ideas	Skills
Literacy	• Hero's journey theme • Memoir • Sometimes we can use stories to understand our own lives • Words and pictures together can tell a story • Stories often show conflicts	• Summarizing the action • Identifying the main idea • Expressing ideas clearly • Point of view
Social and Emotional Learning	• Conflict is a natural part of life • Conflicts can have solutions where everyone is happy • Even if conflicts cannot be solved, we can always take some action to make things better • Listening to others helps us find ways to solve problems • We can get what we want without resorting to violence	• Brainstorming solutions to conflicts • Win-win negotiation • The ABCDE model for problem solving • De-escalating conflicts • Mediation

Brothers in Hope: The Story of the Lost Boys of Sudan, by Mary Williams; illustrated by R. Gregory Christie. Lee and Low Books Inc., 2005

SUMMARY

The author has taken stories of survivors of an incredible trek and woven them into a tale of courage, hope, and problem-solving. We meet eight-year-old Garang as his father has told him that he is old enough to care for the family's wealth, its cattle. He is afraid, for the cattle are much bigger than he. His father urges him to "be brave. Your heart and mind are strong. There is nothing you cannot do." These words will guide him as he faces both two-footed and four-footed dangers ahead.

War comes to his village, and only the boys who were in the fields tending cattle survive the slaughter. As Garang wanders, stunned, he meets other boys who have also lost everything. "We were children, not used to caring for ourselves. Without our parents we were lost. We had to learn to take care of one another."

They pick leaders and form groups, adopting what we would call a "buddy" system, then set off toward the east and Ethiopia. Garang is in charge of a group as well as of a five-year-old named Chuti.

After a grueling trip in which they deal with fear, hunger, and wild animals, they cross into Ethiopia, where they meet an aid worker named Tom, who offers them food and shelter. They go to school.

Then, just "when it seemed things were finally okay for us," war forces them back to their homeland. They endure another harrowing journey before miraculously meeting up with Tom again and settling in a refugee camp.

Tom is returning to the United States to raise money and awareness. He asks Garang to tell him his story. After holding so much in to be brave in front of the others, Garang "talked all day and all night. . . . After telling my story, the storm of war no longer seemed as scary. The thunder was not as loud."

Tom leaves, life becomes harder. The group maintains its solidarity, even though many are so weak from hunger that they can no longer go to school. They solve the problem by taking "turns foraging for food and going to school." Those who were at school would share their lessons at night with those who had foraged and would share their food. In this way, "we were able to feed our bodies and our minds."

Years pass. Garang is twenty-one years old when Tom returns. Tom announces that the United States will now allow the Sudanese young men to emigrate. Garang is thrilled but also scared: "I wondered if people in America would accept me. . . .I thought it might be better to stay. . .

As always, he returns to his father's words: "Your heart and mind are strong. There is nothing you cannot do." He reflects that as a child he did not really understand what his father had said, but now "my heart was strong. . . . I was no longer afraid. I would find the strength to make a new life."

The book ends on a note of hope, although a postscript in the author's own voice tells us that life has not been easy for many of the refugees. Their homeland is still torn by war, they are no longer "boys," and they face many challenges.

COMMENT

Although we hope we will never face such extreme situations, we can relate the boys' dilemmas to those of our own lives. (Note: It is possible that some students in the class will have experienced major upheaval in their lives as a result of war and displacement.) We can pinpoint their conflicts and problems as well as our own. The characters in the book could have chosen self-pity, revenge, or war, but they didn't.

We can also see how the author has shaped this semi-fictional story to make it conform to fictional stories with which our students may or may not yet be familiar (think *The Odyssey, Harry Potter, Through the Looking Glass, The Wizard of Oz, The Hunger Games*). Such tales fit into a category of stories often called "the hero's journey," but for our purposes we want to look at the fact that the main character has friends, companions, and mentors who help him in his problem-solving as he encounters myriad obstacles.

We can look to people in our own communities who offer hope and alternatives in the most daunting and dangerous of circumstances. We can look for real-life examples of people who find win-win solutions in the face of overwhelming problems.. We can trace the journey of our own lives and look at problems we have encountered, whether external or internal, and talk about the solutions we came to.

We can talk about how, like the author and like the fictionalized character she created, we have been influenced by others and then passed on the positive influence.

We can do research on what has happened to this group of young men since they came to the United States. We can learn more about current refugee crises in the world.

Book Talk

READ-ALOUD

Previewing the book

Show the covers of the book and ask whether the students can guess what the book is about. Has anyone heard the word "Sudan" before? What clues are on the covers about where the action of the book might take place? Show the map at the back of the book and point to Sudan, Ethiopia, and Kenya. Try to find a map of Africa that will give the students an idea of the distances traveled by the group. Compare the thousand-mile journey to a trip a thousand miles from your classroom. Show such a distance on a map of the United States.

Tell the students that the author of the book works with people who come from other countries to live in the United States. She works with people who come here because of wars in their own countries. She met many young men who came from Sudan, and after she heard their stories she wanted to help them more. She started an organization to help them get more education. She wanted people in the United States to know their story, so she combined several of their accounts into one story. The illustrator dedicates his work to all the children affected by famine, poverty, illness, and ignorance. Do the students know the meaning of these words? Do these words give them a clue about what will happen in the book?

Reading and responding to the book

Read the story. Pause to explain unfamiliar words. There are several points where the book could come to a "happy ending" but doesn't. Pause at those points--such as when the boys cross into Ethiopia, cross the river and find that they have not lost anyone, or find Tom again at the camp in Kenya--and ask the students what they think will happen next.

After you have finished reading the story, ask the students, What would you like to say about this story? Do you have any questions?

Deepening the students' understanding of the book

Ask the students to recall the main events of the story. What themes do they see? Encourage as many ideas and interpretations as you can. There are many ways to look at this work. It is a modern story with a modern sensibility, but it follows some of the conventions of a mythic tale. It could be from the pages of the morning paper or from a Greek myth. The outside dangers, although as monstrous as any encountered by Odysseus, are downplayed in favor of the internal dangers of despair and fear. On one level, it is a straightforward adventure. On another, it is a quest book and a coming-of-age story: Dorothy went to Oz; Arthur searched for the Holy Grail, Odysseus was trying to return home after a war; and numerous other fictional characters have sought something that would, they thought, make their lives complete, only to find that it was the journey itself that brought true rewards. Garang learns that he cannot know whether his life will turn out well, but he knows that as long as he has faith (in this case both in a higher power and in himself) and stays connected to his community he will be able to make a new life wherever he goes. Some students may see similarities between this story and the Exodus story, in which a group wandered in the wilderness for many years. Some students may be immigrants who have made dangerous trips to arrive in the United States. Encourage as many connections as possible, but be sure that the problem-solving aspects are brought out. At every turning point, the boys face a problem. How they deal with that problem affects the rest of the story.

Tell the students that you will read the book again. This time, you want them to notice the problems the boys faced and the ways they solved them. As you read the story a second time, ask students to put up their hands when Garang and the boys were facing a problem. Call on a student to state the problem and the decisions the boys made to address it. For example, early on the boys saw that their group consisted of many children, some as young as five, who didn't know how to take care of themselves. To survive they would have to keep track of each other. So the older boys had a meeting and decided to divide the large group into smaller groups, each headed by an older boy who would be responsible for the boys in his group. .

Other problems include

- how to travel safely in a desert
- how to take care of the very young children
- how to find food
- how to divide food
- whether or not to go to school
- what to do once they are in Ethiopia
- where to go when fighting breaks out in Ethiopia
- how or whether to cross the river into Sudan on the way to Kenya
- what to do in the refugee camp (i.e., sit and be depressed or gain skills and help others)
- how to deal with hunger in the camp
- whether to take a chance on going to the United States

The author of this book has been quoted as saying that she was struck by the lack of bitterness on the part of the "lost boys." She believes that their story of surviving the horrors of war can inspire children facing bullies in the schoolyard. The author herself has endured separation from her parents, assault, and bullying at school. She has written about her life in a memoir. *Brothers in Hope* is a fictional account drawn from several different lives. Our focus here is not on the political situation in Sudan but on young people finding the courage to arrive at creative solutions and take action even in extremely challenging situations.

Connecting the book to students' lives

Pair-share and go round. We all face problems in our lives. After you have re-read the book and discussed the problems faced by the boys, ask the students to pair up and share with their partners a time when they faced a problem and were able to solve it. It can be a big problem like that of the boys in the story or a small, everyday problem. How did they solve it? Did someone help them or did they solve it by themselves?

Send the talking piece around for students to share a problem they faced and how they solved it, if they wish to do so.

Writing: Ask the students to write about the problem they shared in the go-round or about another problem and how they solved it.

Garang's father tells him, "Your heart and mind are strong. There is nothing you cannot do." What are things that you do to make your heart and mind strong?

One of the decisions the group makes to help ensure their survival is to have older boys "adopt" younger boys and take responsibility for them. Have you ever had to be responsible for someone else (such as a younger sibling)? How did having this responsibility affect the decisions you made? Students may want to recall the story *Your Move* (Unit 4) and how James had responsibility for his younger brother Isaac; how did this affect decisions he made?

ROLE-PLAY

Divide the class into groups of four and have each group pick a scene from the book that it will rehearse briefly and then present to the class.

Applied Learning

Lesson 1

Objectives

Students will
- review the definition of conflict and distinguish it from violence
- explore what can be good about conflict
- learn various ways in which conflicts can turn out (win-win, win-lose, and lose-lose)
- generate win-win solutions for a conflict
- explore the difference between positions and needs

Materials

- Agenda on chart paper or the chalkboard
- Chart of "Ways Conflicts Can Turn Out"

Gathering

"If you could go to a peaceful place today, where would you go?" Whether our lives are going along smoothly or we're facing challenges as the boys in the story did, it can be helpful to take a journey in our minds to a place we find peaceful.

Ask the students to talk briefly in pairs. Then give several volunteers a chance to share their peaceful place with the group.

Check agenda

Go over the objectives and the agenda.

Defining "conflict" and distinguishing it from violence

In Unit 3 (Listening) the students did a conflict web and discussed the meaning of the word conflict. Here we want to remind them briefly of our working definition of conflict as an argument, a disagreement, or a fight and to reinforce the distinction between conflict and violence.

On the chalkboard, write CONFLICT = VIOLENCE and say that many people equate the two. Ask, Does conflict = violence? What's the difference between them?

In a conflict, people's needs or wants are clashing in some way. Or they're experiencing strong feelings about a situation or something another person has done. In other words, they are experiencing a problem.

That's very different from violence, in which someone deliberately tries to hurt another person or force them to do something that's not good for them to do. Conflict can lead to violence, but it doesn't have to. In The 4Rs Program, we're learning skills to deal with conflict in creative, peaceful, nonviolent ways.

When you're confident that the class understands the distinction, draw a line through the equals sign (CONFLICT ≠ VIOLENCE) to demonstrate that conflict and violence do not have to go together. When a conflict arises, we have choices; and our choices can be peaceful, nonviolent ones.

Web: What's good about conflict?

Not only is conflict different from violence. Handled well, conflict can lead to positive outcomes. Ask if the students have experienced or witnessed a conflict that led to something good. Give the class a minute of silence to think about this question. Call on a volunteer to share a story, and share of story from your own life of a conflict that had a positive outcome. Then lead the class in creating a web of "What's great about conflict."

Your web might look something like this:

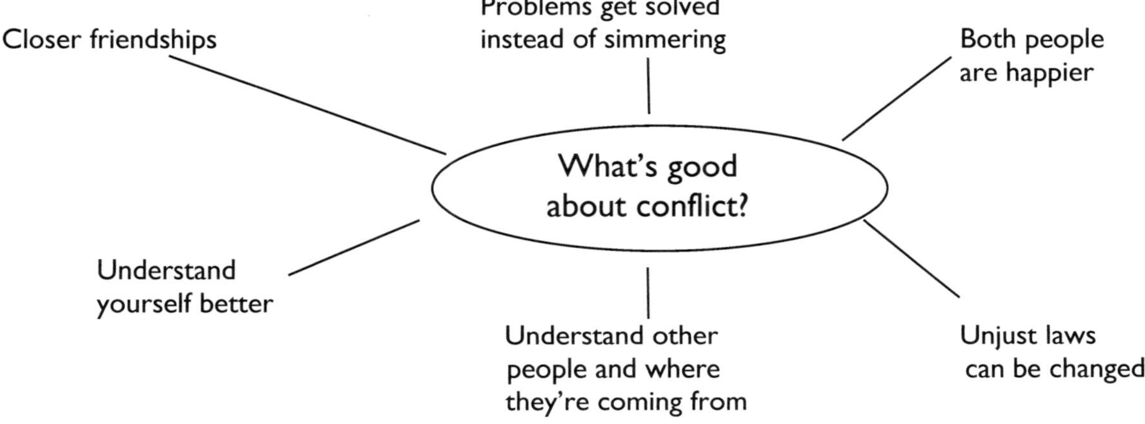

Win-win solutions

Ask the students to work in pairs and to decide who will be Person A and who will be Person B. Explain that you'll give them a situation to role-play. Remind them that in role-plays they must not touch each other. When you clap your hands and say "freeze," they will stop the action and become quiet.

Give the students the following situation or one of your own choosing that you think will be relevant to their lives.

SITUATION: The student wants to buy a pair of expensive sneakers or shoes. The parent or guardian says that what the student has is just fine, and besides, there is no money for such things.

Person A is the student, Person B is the parent or guardian.

Tell students to begin the role-play. Let it run for a minute or two.

Freeze the action.
Ask students what happened in their role-plays? Take several answers. Students will probably describe a variety of behaviors. They may have argued or whined. The adult may have started out calm and then threatened the student if the student wouldn't stop whining. Conversely, the adult may have said yes but clearly been unhappy. They may have begun to work out a solution. Accept all of the students' contributions without judgment. Have them take a few deep abdominal breaths, and begin the role-play.

Ask the students to play the roles again, but this time with the idea that they are each committed to finding a solution that would make them both happy. They will have one minute to come up with a solution. Have them begin the role-play.

When the minute is up, ask the students what solutions they found. It's possible that there will be different solutions: the adult may say that she or he can't afford the shoes right now, but can get them in a few months or if the student can find them on sale; the student may offer to do different chores around the house or come up with some ways to save money on something else so that there will be money for the shoes; they may look at different options and decide on something that the adult can afford but that will also make the student happy, etc.

Next, introduce the students to the chart on the following page which summarizes the ways conflicts can turn out.

Ways Conflicts Can Turn Out

	Person B's needs are met	Person B's needs are not met
Person A's needs are met	Win-Win	Win-Lose
Person A's needs are not met	Lose-Win	Lose-Lose

Explain (or remind the students) that if the conflict gets resolved so that both people feel good, we call it a win-win solution. If one person gets what s/he wants and the other person doesn't, that's a win-lose or lose-win. Ask the students to describe an outcome for the conflict between A and B that would be a win-lose or a lose-win. If the conflict is resolved so that nobody is happy, that's a lose-lose solution. Ask the students to imagine how it might happen that the conflict between A and B would end in a lose-lose situation.

Summarize: As we have seen, you were able to come up with win-win solutions to the conflict between these two people. You have illustrated a very important principle of conflict resolution: Sometimes we can solve conflicts so that both people get what they want.

Positions vs. needs

Explain that if we want to find win-win solutions, we have to understand what the people in the conflict really want. What we <u>really</u> want is called an "underlying need." That means it is something that lies under what we are saying out loud. It is something basic or important that you want or are hoping for. Write "Underlying Need" on the board. For instance, if I'm hungry, I have a need for food. If I'm barefoot in the city or have outgrown my shoes, I have a need for shoes. Now write the word "Position" on the board. A position is one way I can satisfy or meet that need. If I'm hungry, I can eat lots of different kinds of food. The position is the food I've chosen, say fried chicken instead of a hamburger. If I need something on my feet to protect them, I can buy sneakers or boots or sandals. The type of foot covering I want or choose is my position.

Ask the students to look at the conflict between the student and the parent or guardian. What is the student's need? (Is it for new shoes or is it for cool shoes that others will admire?)What is the adult's need? (Is it to be sure there is enough money for everything else the family needs or is it to feel that the student will appreciate the shoes if they're not just a gift?)

As long as we stay with positions, such as "I want those specific shoes" or "We don't have money for fancy shoes" we will have a hard time reaching a win-win solution. If, however, we identify the underlying needs of both parties, we can often find a creative solution to our conflict.

A win-win solution may not always be possible. But when we get into a conflict, it's always a good idea to ask, Is there a way to solve this so that both of us can get what we want? This requires figuring out and focusing on what you really, really want.

Closing

Turn the lights off and give students one minute to close their eyes and revisit the peaceful place they went to in the Gathering for this lesson.

Lesson 2

Objectives

Students will
- be able to define negotiation
- learn a five-step process for conducting win-win negotiation

Materials

- Agenda on chart paper or the chalkboard
- Chart of The Five Ws of Win-Win Negotiation (shown on the next page)
- Copies of the "Negotiation Script" for the two students who will play the characters (see handout at the end of the unit)

> **NOTE**: Before the lesson begins, choose two students to read the Negotiation Script and act out the characters. Give them the script so that they can prepare.

Gathering: Quick, quick, slow

Ask students to stretch their arms above their heads, wiggle their fingers, and then drop their hands quickly into their laps. Repeat a second time. The third time, ask them to lower their hands slowly, taking perhaps 10-15 seconds to lower their hands completely. Do this with the students so that they follow your motions. This exercise encourages physical self-regulation and can be both energizing and calming.

Check agenda

Go over the objectives and the agenda.

Defining negotiation

Write the word "negotiation" on the board and ask the students if they know what it means. Using students' contributions as much as possible, explain that it is a fancy word for "talking things out." Negotiation is a process by which two or more parties talk with each other in order to reach an agreement.

Although we often hear the word negotiation in connection with efforts to settle labor disputes and conflicts between countries, negotiation is something we do every day. Brothers and sisters negotiate over sharing of clothes; friends negotiate over which game to play or movie to see; parents and children negotiate over chores and bedtimes. The boys in the story had a meeting and negotiated an agreement about how they would take care of each other. Any time you talk with someone to try to come to an agreement about something, you're negotiating

Ask the students to give examples of recent negotiations from their own lives.

Introduction to win-win Negotiation

In this lesson, we introduce students to a five-step process of win-win negotiation and give them opportunities to practice. Win-win negotiation is a complex skill that gives the students the opportunity to apply much of what they've been learning in the Applied Learning sections of The 4Rs curriculum, including active listening, assertiveness, and brainstorming.

Present the following situation to the students: a young person and a parent are having a disagreement. One wants to go to a party. The other wants to have a clean house for when grandmother arrives the next day. Explain that we're going to see how they might solve their problem through win-win negotiation.

Show the students the chart below:

The Five Ws of Win-Win Negotiation

1. What's our problem?

2. Where are you coming from?
   (What's your underlying need?)

3. Where am I coming from? (What's my underlying need?)

4. What are some possible win-win solutions?

5. Which one shall we choose?

Explain that when two people are trying for a win-win solution, they need to keep the five questions on the chart in mind. Walk them through the chart, as follows:

- First, you and the other person have to acknowledge that you are having a problem or disagreement.
- Then you both have to put your needs out on the table. Sometimes other people will be clear about their needs. In other cases, it's not so clear; you have to ask and then use active listening to draw them out. It's just as important that you put your own needs out, and that requires assertiveness.
- Once the underlying needs are clear, you have to brainstorm possible solutions that take everyone's needs into account. This requires cooperation and creative thinking. Finally, everyone has to agree on one of the solutions.

To illustrate the process, ask the student actors you have chosen to read the Negotiation Script, acting out a child and adult having a conflict.

> Child: Dee's having a birthday party tomorrow. Can you take me over there?

> Adult: Tomorrow's Saturday. You promised you would clean your room. Grandma will be staying in it when she comes on Sunday.

> Child: But everyone's going to the party, and I don't want to miss it.

> Adult: I won't have my mother staying in a pig pen. You have to clean up.

> Child: I like it when Grandma comes, but I want to go to the party.

> Adult: I don't have time to clean your room, and if I take you to the party, I'll barely have time to clean the whole place.

Stop the dialogue here and ask the students,

- What's the problem? (The child wants to go to the party, but is supposed to clean her/his room, and there is a time pressure. The adult is also feeling time pressure and wants to clean the rest of the house or apartment.)
- Where is the child coming from? What's the need here?
- Where is the adult coming from? What's the need here?
- Ask the students, What are some possible win-win solutions for the child and adult? Elicit the students' ideas.
- Ask, Which one would you choose if you were the people in this situation?

Once the students in the class agree on a possible solution, ask the two students actors to act out the child and adult getting to the solution that the class has agreed on.

Evaluation

Discuss: How do you feel about the solution we came up with for these two characters. Does it seem realistic? Does it really meet both of their needs? Can you see yourself using a process like this to solve problems in your own life?

Closing: Mirroring

Have students face a partner. Decide who will be A and who will be B. A begins by moving in place in any way that feels comfortable. B must observe closely and "mirror" A's movements. After a minute or two, have the students pause and reverse roles. B chooses the movements and A must mirror them.

Ask the students: How can paying attention to another in this way help you become a better negotiator?

Lesson 3

Objective

Students will
- practice win-win negotiation through role-playing

Materials

- Agenda on chart paper or the chalkboard
- Copies of Negotiation Case 1 for Student Role-play (see handout at the end of the unit)

Gathering: Balancing

Ask students to stand. Explain that you are going to try finding different ways to balance. Have students begin by standing on one leg. Then see what happens when you

- bend the knee of your standing leg
- raise and lower the lifted foot
- raise arms overhead, in front of you, to the side, or one arm to the front and one to the back

Encourage student to pay attention to their breathing as they balance. For some people, focusing their gaze on a fixed point on a wall in front of them or on the floor helps them to balance.

Practicing win-win negotiation

In this activity, we follow up on Lesson 2 by giving students a chance to practice win-win negotiation. They will work in groups of three. Two students will be the people negotiating with each other, and the third student will be an observer. The observer's role is to help the negotiators stay on task and to help them if they get stuck.

Start with Negotiation Case 1. Negotiation Case 1 is between two brothers, but by substituting different names, you can turn it into a negotiation between two sisters or a sister and a brother.

The handout is divided into three parts: (1) a brief overview of the dispute, (2) information on the underlying needs of the fourth grader, and (3) information on the underlying needs of the sixth grader.

Here are suggested steps for carrying out the activity with your students:

- Explain that the students are now going to practice The Five Ws of Negotiation
- Group the students into triads
- Distribute copies of the handout The Five Ws of Win-Win Negotiation to all students and walk them through a review of it, calling on various students to explain each of the steps.
- Explain that two of the students will be the people having the conflict and will use The Five Ws to try to talk it out. The third person will be an observer and coach if they get stuck.
- Give the students an overview of the situation by reading to all of the students the first paragraph of the Negotiation Case 1 Handout—the paragraph that describes the Problem or Situation.
- Ask the students to decide who in their group will be the sixth grader, who will be the fourth grader, and who will be the observer. The role of the observer will be to keep the negotiators on task and help them if they get stuck.
- Once students in all of the groups have decided which character they'll play, ask all of the students who are playing the fourth grader to meet with you in a corner of the room or a minute or two. Referring to the handout, read them the description of the fourth grader's underlying needs, keeping your voice low so that only those playing the fourth grader can hear you. Do they have any questions? Do they understand the character they will be playing?
- Now call the students who will be playing the sixth grader to meet with you for a minute or two and read them the description of the underlying needs for that character.
- With everyone back in their triads, ask if anyone has any questions.
- Remind them to look for times in the role-play when they might be able to use Plan 1-2-3 to good advantage. Briefly review Plan 1-2-3 and ask, "Why might Plan 1-2-3 be useful when you're trying to talk out a conflict with somebody? When might it be useful? Discuss briefly.
- Tell them to start.

Give them about 3-5 minutes to complete the negotiation. Give a few minutes for the observers to give feedback and discuss the negotiation with the negotiators. Then ask the observers to share what happened in their group with the class.

Evaluation

Discuss: How did it go? What solution did the negotiators come up with? Was it easy? Difficult? Why? Were the negotiators able to put their needs on the table? Did they listen well to each other? Did anyone get stuck? If so, did the observer help you get "unstuck"? If so, how? Can you see using a process like this to settle disagreements in your own life?

> **NOTE**: To give the students additional practice, we have provided a second hand-out, Negotiation Case 2. You can create your own cases, and you can ask your students to do so as well.

Closing

Close with a round of applause for you and the class for working hard on a challenging topic.

Lesson 4

Objective

Students will
- practice a basic problem-solving method by tackling an actual classroom problem

Materials

- Agenda on chart paper or the chalkboard
- Chart paper, markers, masking tape
- Chart paper with the A B C D E method of problem solving (p. 120)

Gathering: Alphabet soup

Tell the students that you will shout out a letter from A to E and they will respond popcorn style with a word that starts with that letter. Encourage every student to participate.

Check agenda

Go over the objective and agenda

Problem solving

The ABCDE approach to problem solving, conceived by William Kreidler, is a useful way to introduce young people to creative problem-solving methods. Here we use the ABCDE approach to solve a class problem.

Choose a problem or issue that has been plaguing your class (for example, students keep losing their pencils, squabbles break out daily at clean-up time, or a lot of tattling is going on). If you prefer, you can ask the class to brainstorm a list of problems and then guide them through a process of choosing one to focus on. If the class generates a list, you can ask them to vote on which is the most important and keep dropping the ones with the least votes. Each student gets one vote on each round of voting.

Then address the problem as follows:

<u>A</u>sk, What's the problem? Give the students a chance to talk about the problem and how it affects them. As students speak about the problem, encourage others in the class to listen with full presence and awareness, give the speaker focused attention, fully take in what she/he is saying, and listen for underlying needs or concerns.

<u>B</u>rainstorm solutions. The guidelines for brainstorming are as follows: (1) Set a time limit of several minutes; (2) Encourage the group to put out lots of ideas; (3) Record the ideas on a chart or the chalkboard; (4) Don't discuss or judge any idea. The ideas don't need to be "realistic." Sometimes, a "wild" idea can lead to a creative solution.

<u>C</u>hoose one. Discuss the ideas. Talk about the consequences of carrying out various ideas. Which have the best chance of working to solve the problem? Guide the class through a process of choosing one to try.

<u>D</u>o it! The only way we'll know for sure if it's a good idea is to try it. Set a time limit — long enough to give the idea a good trial, short enough to limit the damage if the idea doesn't work.

<u>E</u>valuate. When the time limit is up, usually in a week or so, meet to see how effective the idea has been in addressing the problem. In some cases, you may need to tinker with the idea to make it fully effective. In other cases, you may decide to go back to the drawing board. If the idea worked, congratulations! Now you can move on to tackle another problem.

When you're done, debrief with the students. How was this process for us? Do you think we came up with a good solution? Would you recommend using the process again?

If you and the class find the process useful, have class meetings for problem solving on a regular basis or use ABCDE problem solving whenever problems come up. Your students will be applying The 4Rs skills they're learning to solve real-life problems.

Closing

Lead the class in the following cheer:

A B C D E you see

Problem solved by you and me!

Lesson 5

Objectives

Students will get an introduction to the skill of de-escalating conflicts

Materials

- Agenda on chart paper

- Copies of the handout "Conflict: Going Up the Escalator, Going Down the Escalator" for the students.

Gathering

Give the students an opportunity to practice their deep (abdominal) breathing (as introduced in Unit 2). Point out that deep breathing can help them calm and center themselves. It's a skill that's especially useful in dealing with conflict.

Turn off the lights and sit in a chair in front of the students. Ask them to do what you do. Put the palm of your hand on your abdomen. Breathe in deeply and slowly while expanding your belly and chest. Then breathe out slowly, contracting your belly.

Do five cycles, each cycle consisting of one breath in and one breath out. Remind them that when they slowly breathe in (belly expanding), they can silently think, "In…" When they slowly breathe out (belly contracting), they can silently think, "Out…"

With the lights still off, ask, How was that for you? Was it easy to breathe in with your belly expanding and out with it contracting? Did anything come into your mind as you were doing this? Did you find it relaxing?

Check agenda

Go over the objective and agenda for the session.

De-escalating conflict

Remind the students of Plan 1-2-3. Ask, What are the three parts of Plan 1-2-3? Elicit that they are Stop, Breathe, Think. In Unit 2 of The 4Rs we practiced applying Plan 1-2-3 to a couple of situations. Today we have a chance to see how we can use Plan 1-2-3 to prevent conflicts from getting out of hand.

Distribute copies of the Conflict Escalation Script to the students. Give them a minute to read it over, then ask for two volunteers to take the parts of the two characters in the script.

Here's the script:

Student A: *[has just been bumped in the hallway by Student B]*

               Hey, you idiot! Watch where you're going!

Student B: *[turns, thrusts his or her face toward Student A, and speaks loudly and angrily]*

               Who're you calling an idiot?

Student A: I'm calling YOU an idiot! *[jabs index finger toward Student B].*

               Watch where you're going!

Student B:		Say that again, and I'll rearrange your face.

Student A:		Let me see you try it, i-di-ot!

Ask the students what they think is likely to happen next.

Explain that this is an example of what we call "going up the conflict escalator."

The students are no doubt familiar with escalators in office buildings or department stores. We can use the idea of the escalator to talk about conflict. When a conflict starts small and then people do things that make them angrier and angrier, we say they are "going up the conflict escalator." If they gradually calm down, we say that they "going down the conflict escalator."

By using Plan 1-2-3—by stopping for a moment, taking a couple of deep breaths, and thinking—the students in this skit might have been able to go down the escalator instead of up the escalator.

Draw a diagram of an escalator going up, as follows:

UP

Draw an escalator going down, as follows:

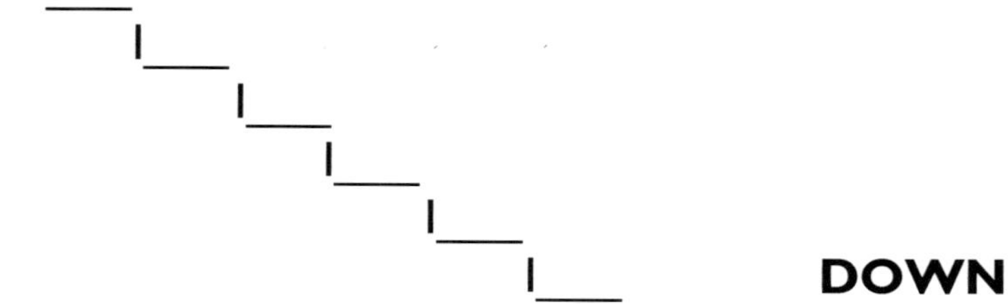

DOWN

Ask the students to identify the "trigger actions or words" that escalate the conflict in the script and chart them as follows:

<u>Try it!</u>

<u>threat</u> |

<u>idiot, finger jab</u> |

<u>"Who. . ."</u>|

<u>idiot</u> |

UP   <u>bump</u> |

Ask the students what either of the characters could have done to come down the escalator or avoid getting on it in the first place. Elicit the students' ideas.

Distribute the handout, "Conflict: Going Up the Escalator, Going Down the Escalator" to the students. At the bottom of the page are ideas for de-escalating conflict. Ask if they think any of those ideas would be helpful in the situation portrayed in the script.

Ask, Where does Plan 1-2-3 enter in? Elicit that it gives us a few moments to calm down and think BEFORE we react. In that time, we may be able to come up with things to say or do that can keep the conflict from escalating. Those few moments can make the difference between a passing incident ("Please watch where you're going!"/"I'm sorry") and a huge fight that leads to people getting hurt and getting into trouble.

Ask the students, Have you ever gone up the conflict escalator? When? What happened? Have you ever gone down the conflict escalator? Did someone help you or did you do it yourself? Call on a couple of students to share their stories with the group.

Now ask the students to work in pairs to create a dialogue between two people who are going up the conflict escalator (that is, having a conflict in which they are getting angrier and angrier at each other). Ask them to chart the dialogue on the UP escalator on the handout, as you did with the scripted example on the board.

After they've charted the escalating conflict, they should find a point at which one of the characters could use Plan 1-2-3 to come up with a smart way to handle the situation—for example, by doing something to change the energy and bring them both people down the escalator. They should mark an X by that step on the escalator and below the escalator write what the person might do or say to start the escalator going down.

Ask several pairs to share the dialogues they have created with the group. Where did they put their X? What did the person do or say to start the escalator going down?

Evaluation

Can the students see using Plan 1-2-3 to help them de-escalate conflicts in real-life situations? Why? Why not? Do they think that the ideas on the handout for de-escalating conflict would be useful in real-life conflicts? Why? Why not? Call on a couple of students to share their thoughts.

Closing

Turn off the lights and give students a minute or two to take several deep breaths while picturing in their minds their peaceful places.

Lesson 6

This is an optional advanced lesson that will take about an hour. Through the lesson, students will get an introduction to mediation and practice the steps of a simple mediation process.

Objectives

Students will
- be able to define mediation, describe the role of the mediator, and identify the qualities that make for a good mediator;
- learn the steps of informal mediation;
- practice informal mediation.

Materials

- Agenda on chart paper or the chalkboard
- Chart paper and marker for recording students' ideas about the qualities of a good mediator
- Copies of "Steps for Mediation" for the students (see the handout at the end of the unit)
- Copies of "Mediation Case 1" for the students (see the handout at the end of the unit)

Gathering: Stand up

In the "Stand up" game, students stand if what you say applies to them. For example, you might say, "Stand up if you're wearing sneakers." Have them sit down and then move onto the next "Stand up." Invent your own "Stand ups" tailored to your class.
Here are a few to get you started:

- Stand up if you're the oldest in your family
- Stand up if you're youngest in your family
- Stand up if you like ice cream
- Stand up if you speak another language besides English
- Stand up if you think adults make too many rules for children

For some stand ups, you may want to ask a couple of volunteers to say more about the topic.

Check agenda

Go over the objectives and the agenda.

Introduction to mediation

Write the word "mediator" on the board and ask the students what it means. If there's a mediation program in the school, the children may be familiar with the word. If not, you may need to explain that a mediator is someone who helps people solve a conflict. Today we're going to learn more about mediation and how we can sometimes be effective as mediators in our everyday lives.

Arrange for two student volunteers to role-play a simple conflict (for example, a dispute over a pencil). Freeze the action with both parties grabbing for the pencil.

Ask: If you were going to try to help these people resolve their conflict, what would you do? Elicit the students' ideas.

Remind the students that *negotiation* is two or more people trying to resolve a conflict by talking it out. If the people in the conflict decide they need help, they may call in another person to help them talk with each other. That's *mediation*. This other person is called a *mediator*. A mediator doesn't take sides or tell the people what to do or decide who's right or wrong. A mediator helps the parties in the conflict talk to each other, and tries to help them come up with a solution they can feel good about.

Ask the students to think of qualities a good mediator would need to have. You might give the students a minute or two to note one or two qualities on a piece of paper before asking them to share their ideas with the class. Record the students' ideas on chart paper.

Students are likely to mention that good listening skills are important for mediators. If so, encourage the class to recall what they have learned in The 4Rs that may help them listen effectively. Point out that mediators may use techniques such as abdominal breathing (introduced in Unit 2) to help them stay calm and focused.

Steps of mediation

Pass out the handout of the Steps for Mediation and walk the students through it as follows:

Ask, Would you like me to help you solve this problem?

Explain that if you see two people having a conflict and you want to help them, the first thing to do is to ask the people if they want your help. You can't force people to take part in mediation. Both sides have to want it. If they both want your help, say that you'd be glad to serve as a mediator. That means you'll ask questions, listen, and help them talk with each other. You won't take sides or tell them what to do. They'll decide how to solve their problem; you'll help them talk with each other.

Go over the rules of mediation.

The next step is to tell them the rules. You might say something like, "Mediation works best if the two of you will agree to some rules. The rules are no interrupting, no name calling, and be as honest as you can."

Ask one person, What happened? Paraphrase.

Ask whether that person agrees with the paraphrase or wants to add anything.

Repeat with the second person.

Once both people have agreed to the rules, then the mediation can begin. This is where the questioning, listening, and paraphrasing come in. Ask, "Who wants to speak first?" Then ask that person, "What happened?" While the person explains what happened from his point of view, listen carefully. When the person is done, paraphrase what you heard. Then ask the other person what happened, listen, and paraphrase.

By now you should have a pretty good idea of what happened and what the conflict is about. If there are still things you don't understand, ask more questions and paraphrase again. If, at any point in the mediation, the two people express strong emotions such as anger, you can suggest that they take a deep breath or two to help them calm down and stay focused on the mediation process.

Ask, what could you have done differently? Paraphrase.

Ask whether the person agrees with the paraphrase or wants to add anything.

Repeat with the other person.

When you're satisfied that you understand what's going on and that the important issues are on the table, it's time to ask each person another question: "Is there something you could have done differently?" The purpose of this question is to get people thinking about whether they have done anything to contribute to the conflict. Again, after each person's response, be sure to paraphrase what you hear and ask whether you have paraphrased correctly.

Ask, what can you do now to solve the problem? Paraphrase.

Repeat with other person.

After both people have explored that question, it's time for another question: "What can you do now to solve the problem?" Again, paraphrase their responses and help them work toward a solution.

If they succeed in coming up with a solution, shake their hands to congratulate them.

If they don't succeed, tell them you appreciate that they were willing to try mediation and that they worked hard to solve the problem (if you feel they did make a good effort). You might ask them what they plan to do next (for example, ask for the teacher's help or have a cooling off period in which they stay away from each other for awhile).

Referring to the handout, summarize by saying that being a good mediator is about watching your LPQs: L for Listen, P for Paraphrase, and Q for Question.

Mediation practice

Divide the students into groups of four. Give them a few minutes to review the steps on the handout you just went over with them. Explain that in each group you want them to agree on two students to be disputants (the ones having the conflict), one person to be the mediator, and one person to be the observer.

Pass out the handout for Mediation Case 1 to each of the observers. The observers share the information on the handout with the disputants and the mediator as instructed by the handout.

Give the students 5-10 minutes to practice the mediation process in their small groups. Tell them that the purpose is to practice; therefore, the disputants should be realistic but not make resolution impossible. If time permits (or on another day), switch roles in the small groups and do the role-play again with the same case (or with Mediation Case 2 (see handout at the end of the lesson) so that other students get a chance to be the mediator. Once your students are on their way to mastering the process, they might try Mediation Case 3 (see handout at the end of the lesson) which is especially challenging. Or make up a mediation case of your own involving issues relevant to your class.

Discuss: How did the mediation go? For those who were disputants: Did you feel the mediator was fair? Listened well? Asked good questions?   For the mediator: Was it easy or difficult to be a mediator? Why? What did you do to manage the challenges of being a mediator? For the observer: What did you appreciate about the way the mediator tried to help the disputants? Do you have any suggestions about what the mediator might do differently next time?

> **NOTE**: You may want to spend additional periods giving the students opportunities to practice mediation. If you train your students to be mediators, they may be able to help resolve some of the conflicts that arise in your class.

Evaluation

Ask the class if they can see themselves actually using mediation in their lives? Why? Why not? Under what circumstances?

Closing

Lead the students in a round of applause for their hard work.

Additional Activities

"We Can Work It Out"

Your students may enjoy hearing the Beatles' song, "We Can Work It Out," and noting the obvious connections between the lyrics and this unit on problem solving.

Find the song on YouTube and play it for the students. Google the lyrics and make copies or project the lyrics on a white board, and have the students sing along.

Make time for silence

During this time the lights are off. No writing, drawing, reading, no gadgets. Just sitting. Encourage students to put their hands on their knees. Students can close their eyes if they want. You can tell them that they can let their minds use the silence as they wish. Or you can suggest ways they might use the silence. For example, they could

- practice abdominal breathing (introduced in Unit 2)
- simply pay attention to their breathing
- pay attention to sounds they hear in their mind or take themselves to a peaceful place
- recall a time they had fun
- recall something they like to do

After the time of silence, ask for a couple of volunteers to share where their minds went during the time. Make time for silence every day, preferably at the same time, such as after lunch or recess or as the first and last actions of the day.

By giving students the opportunity to experience time for silence on a daily basis, you'll be instilling a habit that will serve them well for the rest of their lives.

Consider having your students keep a 4Rs journal

Writing (drawing for younger students) is an excellent way to reinforce and consolidate learning. A journal enables students to put all of their Book Talk writing in one place. You can also give them a few minutes after each 4Rs lesson to jot down a few thoughts about what they're taking away or how they're planning to use what they've just learned. If a student tries a new skill, s/he might want to write about what happened. Did it bring a positive result? If a student is stuck in a conflict with someone, s/he might want to do some writing to sort it out and imagine some solutions. You can give them standard journals and encourage them to decorate them.

By having students keep journals, you will be introducing them to a habit or practice that can serve them well the rest of their lives.

Class meetings for problem solving

In this kind of class meeting the teacher empowers students, facilitating a process by which students apply the skills they're developing through 4Rs lessons to real-life situations in the classroom and the school. By now, your students should have the foundational skills (managing feelings, listening, assertiveness) to be good problem solvers. They have been introduced to the ABCDE problem-solving model, an approach they can grasp easily. A free downloadable copy of Morningside Center's comprehensive guide *Class Meetings for Problem Solving* is available by request.

Related Books

Just Plain Fancy by Patricia Polacco

A Party in Ramadan, by Asma Mobin-Uddin

Tuck Everlasting by Natalie Babbitt

Magid Fasts for Ramadan

Charlotte's Web by E.B White

A great book for young readers on life in the Sudan during the country's civil war and now:

A Long Walk to Water by Newberry Medalist Linda Sue Park

Negotiation Practice Script

Child: Dee's having a birthday party tomorrow.
         Can you take me over there?

Adult: Tomorrow's Saturday. You promised you would clean
         your room. Grandma will be staying in it when she comes
         on Sunday.

Child: But everyone's going to the party, and I don't want to
         miss it.

Adult: I won't have my mother staying in a pig pen.
         You have to clean up.

Child: I like it when Grandma comes, but I want to
         go to the party.

Adult: I don't have time to clean your room, and if I take you
         to the party, I'll barely have time to clean the apartment.

The Five Ws of Win-Win Negotiation

1. What's our problem?

2. Where are you coming from?
    (What's your underlying need?)

3. Where am I coming from?
    (What's my underlying need?)

4. What are some possible win-win solutions?

5. Which one shall we choose?

Negotiation Case 1

The Problem or the Situation

Joe and Ted are brothers. Joe is in fourth grade and Ted is in sixth grade. It's Friday morning, and both boys are getting ready for school. Ted asks if he can borrow the baseball hat Joe got for his birthday the week before.

Ted's Underlying Needs or Concerns

Ted really likes the hat, and it fits him. It looks cool. Even though hats aren't allowed in school, he can wear it before going inside and, especially, he can wear it before the dance after school. All his closest friends will be there, as well as a girl he hopes to impress. Ted has caps of his own, but Joe's is newer and cooler. He wants something special for today.

Joe's Underlying Needs or Concerns

Joe wasn't planning to wear the cap today. He likes Ted and wants to please him, but he's not sure about this. The school is strict about the no-cap rule. What if a teacher takes the cap away from Ted? Plus, Ted's not always very careful about what he borrows. This was a nice gift from a friend. Joe is planning to wear it on Saturday. He wants to be sure he has it to wear tomorrow.

Handout 4 ◆ Unit 5

Negotiation Case 2

The Problem or Situation

Nora and Lyana are sisters. Nora is 9 years old and Lyana is 12. Last year they were in the same school, and Lyana looked out for Nora. They walked back and forth to school together. This year, Lyana has new friends and a lot more homework. Nora wants to spend more time with her, but Lyana is always texting or online with her new friends or doing homework. Recently, Lyana promised to do some things with Nora and has broken her promise. This has made Nora very angry.

Nora's Underlying Needs or Concerns

Nora misses Lyana a lot now that Lyana's in middle school. She wants to spend time with her. She knows that Lyana really likes her, but she doesn't like it when Lyana promises to do something and then breaks her promise.

She understands that her sister has lots of homework and new friends, but she still wants to keep the special sister relationship she has with her.

Lyana's Underlying Needs or Concerns

Lyana loves her sister, but she's feeling under a lot of stress. It hasn't been easy to make new friends. There's a lot more homework. She wishes her sister wouldn't bug her and make her feel guilty. She wishes her sister would understand how stressful things are for her.

Handout 5 • Unit 5

A B C D E
Problem-Solving Method

Ask, What's the problem?

Brainstorm solutions.

Choose one.

Do it!

Evaluate. After about a week, check in to see how the solution is working.

* Adapted from *Teaching Conflict Resolution Through Children's Literature* by William Kreidler.

Conflict Escalation Script

Student A: [has just been *bumped in the hallway by Student B]*

Hey, you idiot! Watch where you're going!

Student B: *[turns, thrusts his or her face toward Student A, and speaks loudly and angrily]*

Who're you calling an idiot?

Student A: I'm calling YOU an idiot!

[jabs an index finger toward Student B]

Watch where you're going!

Student B: Say that again and I'll rearrange your face.

Student A: Let me see you try it, i-di-ot!

Handout 7 • Unit 5

Conflict:
Going Up the Escalator, Going Down the Escalator

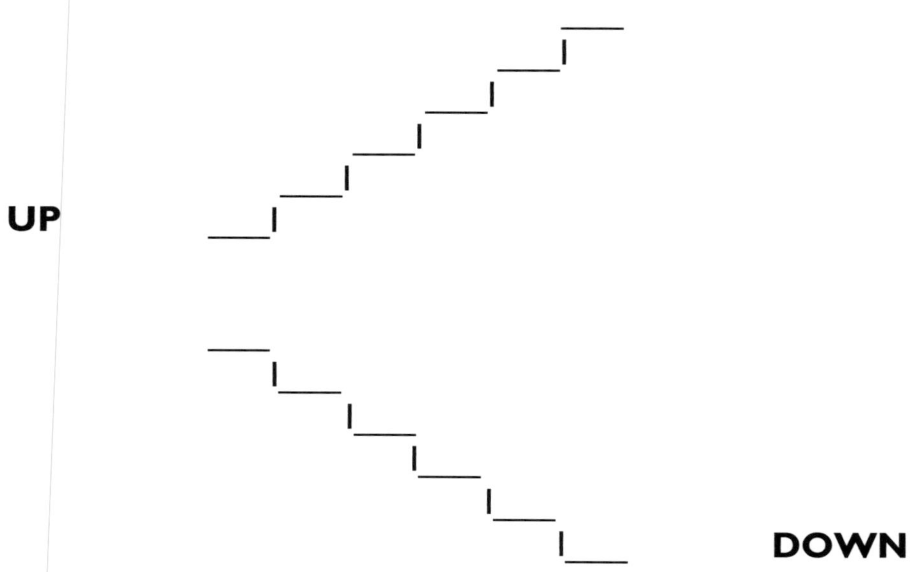

Example of how to chart the conflict portrayed in the script

Some ways to de-escalate a conflict
- Use Plan 1-2-3 to give yourself a moment to think.
- Avoid calling the other person a name even if they called you a name.
- If you did something that upset the other person, say you're sorry.
- If the other person is angry with you, consider validating their feeling. ("I can understand why you feel that way.")
- Avoid jumping to conclusions. Give the other person the benefit of the doubt
- If you didn't mean to upset or inconvenience the other person, say so.

What do you think of these ideas? Can you add other ideas to the list?

Handout 8 • Unit 5

Steps for Mediation

Ask, Would you like me to help you solve this problem?

If both parties agree that they want your help, go over the rules:

- No interrupting
- No name calling
- Be as honest as you can

Ask one person, What happened? Paraphrase. Ask whether the person agrees with your paraphrasing.
Repeat with the second person.

Ask, What could you have done differently? Paraphrase. Ask whether the person agrees with your paraphrasing.
Repeat with other person.

Ask, What can you do now to solve the problem? Paraphrase. Ask whether the person agrees with your paraphrasing.
Repeat with other person.

Help them come to a solution.

Congratulate them on their hard work.

Watch your L P Q s!

LISTEN   PARAPHRASE   QUESTION

Mediation Case 1

<u>Information for the observer and the mediator:</u>

The mediator is on the playground. Two first graders are yelling at each other, calling each other names.

<u>Information only for the disputants:</u>

The two of you were playing a running and chasing game. Student 1 was chasing Student 2. When Student 1 caught up with Student 2, she tagged him. In tagging him, she accidentally pushed him so that he fell, tearing his pants and scraping his knee.

"I'm sorry," Student 1 said, and offered to help him up.

But Student 2 brushed away her hand. "Stupid! Why did you push me? I'm gonna get you now." Student 1 ran away, and Student 2 chased her. When Student 2 caught up with her, they started yelling at each other.

Mediation Case 2

<u>Information for the observer and the mediator:</u>

The mediator is on the playground. Two kindergarteners are arguing loudly over the seesaw.

<u>Information only for the disputants (Student 2 & Student 3):</u>

Student1, Student 2 and Student 3 are friends. You like to play together. Most of the time, it goes fine. But today someone got the idea of playing on the seesaw. The three of you ran to the seesaw.

Student 1 got there first and got on one end. Student 2 and Student 3 got to the other end of the seesaw about the same time. Student 2 pushed Student 3 away and climbed on the seesaw.

Student 3, angry that his friend had pushed him away, yelled, "Get off! I got here first," and started pushing Student 2 off the seesaw.

It quickly became a pushing and shouting match with both students calling each other names.

Mediation Case 3

Information for the disputants and the mediator:

It's lunchtime. You're in the cafeteria. You notice that two good friends of yours who usually sit together are pouting and sitting apart. You ask one of them what's going on and s/he says, "We're not friends anymore. I'll never be his/her friend after what s/he did."

Information only for Student 1:

Yesterday you came to school feeling very upset. You had just learned that your parents are splitting up. As if that isn't bad enough, they're arguing over who will have custody of you. If your father gets custody, you'll have to move from the neighborhood and attend a different school. You said there's no way you'll go to live with your father. You'll run away from home first.

You shared this information and your feelings with your best friend, Student 2. You made it very clear that this was confidential. You made your friend promise not to tell anybody. You didn't say anything to anybody else.

Today when you came to school, the teacher asked to talk with you. It was clear that she knew everything about your situation. Later, another student in the class said, "I'm sorry to hear about your parents." You are furious at your friend for betraying your confidence.

Mediation Case #3, *continued*

Information only for Student 2:

Yesterday when you came to school, you could see that your best friend, Student1, was very upset. It was clear s/he'd been crying. You asked what was wrong. S/he told you that s/he had just learned that his/her parents are splitting up. Even more upsetting, they are arguing over who will have custody of the children. Your friend (Student1) said that if his/her father gets custody (which would mean leaving the neighborhood and going to another school), s/he'll run away before going to live with him. Your friend told you that all of this was strictly confidential. You mustn't tell anyone.

You promised not to tell anyone and you fully intended to keep your promise. But you were very upset by what your friend told you. And you were worried—about his/her leaving the school, about the threat to run away.

That afternoon, while Student 1 was out of the classroom doing a special project with the art teacher, you started to cry. The teacher asked you what was wrong and you couldn't stop yourself from telling her. Some of the other children must have noticed what was going on and overheard your conversation with the teacher.

You're sorry you didn't keep your promise, but the friendship means a lot to you, and you care about your friend.

Blank by design.

5

Unit 6 Theme

*Celebrating Diversity &
Countering Discrimination*

Unit 6 Book Selection

Friends from the Other Side by Gloria Anzaldua
Children's Book Press, 1993

Activities

- Culture Web
- Culture Banners
- Prejudice and Discrimination
- First Thoughts: Exploring Stereotypes
- Four Behaviors in Bully Situations
- What We Can Do
- Standing Up Against Discrimination [Skits]
- *Additional Activities*

Introduction

We live in a multi-cultural, multi-racial society, but even if we lived in a mono-cultural one, we would discover numerous differences among us.

In this unit, students will look at the ways that everyone is different while at the same time being part of the human community. They will read stories in which characters are targeted for being "different." In some stories, the community realizes after it is too late how it could have been enriched if it had accepted the person. In other stories, characters gain inner strength to stand up to being targeted, while in others the community bands together against those who target the individual. The key point is that we are all different, and that is totally OK. We do not need to feel bad about ourselves because we don't seem to fit a norm. We do not need to make ourselves feel superior by putting someone else down. Our classroom and our larger community are stronger and better because we each bring different strengths to them.

There is no place in our classroom or in society for putting down or mistreating others because they are "different." Research shows that children as young as three and four can see differences and pick up cues about responding from the older people around them. The lessons for pre-K through first grade focus on acknowledging similarities and differences among people and accepting them.

In grades two through five, the lessons continue to emphasize acknowledging and celebrating diversity. In these grades we also address the shadow side of diversity, the ways in which difference is used as an excuse for teasing and bullying. Teasing and bullying exist in classrooms where everyone is the same age and from the same ethnic group. The "differences" can be height, weight, wearing glasses, gender, hair color, having the "wrong" clothes, or social class, to name a few. In multi-ethnic classrooms, aggressors may seize on perceived racial, religious, or cultural differences.

Whatever reasons aggressors pick for targeting individuals, not one is valid. Our school communities need to be based on respect for all. Bullying has no place in the school. In grades two through five, we define bullying and identify four roles people play in bullying situations:

- Aggressor
- Target
- Bystander
- Ally

As we address bullying in the older grades, teachers need to keep in mind that not all aggression is bullying. A fight between two evenly matched opponents may be against school rules, but it is not bullying. A shouting match between two verbally adept students may be unpleasant and unnecessary, but it is not bullying. **Bullying always involves a real or perceived power imbalance**. The person who bullies does it because he or she can. Students who bully don't pick on people who will resist successfully. We define bullying as a repeated pattern of aggression intended to hurt another person, either physically or emotionally. It's not only physical: words do hurt. In addition, with the Internet, bullying can be carried on from a distance and anonymously.

This unit will begin to give students tools to understand and accept difference and to combat bullying. Students in the older grades will learn that in addition to understanding the behavior of those who bully and the responses of those who are targeted, bystanders and allies have roles to play too. For every student who bullies there are many bystanders. They are literally people who are on the scene, standing by. Every bystander has the potential to become an ally, either by offering support to the targeted person afterward, standing up to the person who bullies, or getting help from a trusted adult. Ultimately, it's the bystanders, not those doing the bullying, who have the power — if they choose to use it.

Studies show that students have very little confidence in adults to help them in such situation, and, unfortunately, they are right. Too many adults either don't see the bullying in front of their eyes or don't understand how devastating bullying is to the target and how harmful it is to the learning environment.

Students who bully often defend their actions with such phrases as, "I was just kidding" or "Can't you take a joke?" Of course, there is teasing among friends, but friends stop at or just after they cross the line. Students who bully don't. Adults are not always able to distinguish between playful teasing and harmful teasing.

Although the legal ramifications of bullying are not covered in this unit, teachers should be aware that many states have anti-harassment and anti-bullying legislation. When students who have been targeted or their families have sued, school districts have been held liable for not preventing or stopping bullying that has caused the target to suffer emotional damage, transfer to another school, or commit suicide. In addition, both students and teachers need to know what the discipline code for their school district is. Students may not realize how stiff the penalties can be for bullying.

In this unit

		Ideas	Skills
	Literacy	• Stories can be imagined from real life • Authors may imagine stories from incidents or memories from their own lives • Writers use description and dialogue to make us feel that we are in the story • We can learn a lot about culture from fiction, but we have to check it against nonfiction references • Conflicts in a story can be between characters or between people and institutions	• Identifying the main idea • Asking questions • Expressing ideas clearly • Providing evidence to back up one's assertions • Interviewing • Researching
	Social and Emotional Learning	• We can learn to understand and appreciate people who are different from us • Culture is a set of traditions, beliefs, and practices common to a group of people • It's our responsibility to stand up to discrimination	• Understanding and appreciating our own and other people's cultures • Identifying various kinds of systematic mistreatment of groups of people • Recognizing and countering stereotypes • Standing up to discrimination

Friends from the Other Side, by Gloria Anzaldua, illus. by Consuelo Mendez. Children's Book Press, 1993. Bilingual.

SUMMARY

Prietita is sitting on a tree branch in her backyard when she spies Joaquin, who had come to the gate to sell firewood. She notices that he wears a long-sleeved shirt in the hot South Texas climate. She notices that his Spanish differsfrom hers. She asks if he comes from " 'the other side. . . .You know, from Mexico?'" Yes, he answersshyly, tugging at the sleeves of his shirt. When he picks up the wood to leave, she noticesthe boils on his arms and realizes that he is ashamed of the sores. Immediately she thinks that the herb woman can help him. But Joaquin hurries away before she can say anything.

Soon she hears neighborhood children yelling and goes to the gate to see what is happening. Her cousin Tete is the ringleader. "'Look at the mojadito, *look at the wetback!'" he cries. Prietita "felt her body go stiff." She hesitates slightly, "pulled between her new friend and her old friends," but when one of the boys picks up a rock she knows what to do. She runs in front of Joaquin and scolds the boys. Her cousin sneers, "'Who asked you to butt in, Prietita?'" His friends pull him back, and the boys saunter away, "acting as though they had chosen to leave." From this encounter, Prietita and Joaquin forge a friendship. She appears to be a little older than he is, so she offers to walk him home after this frightening experience.*

Home is a "tumbledown shack" with a tarp where one wall should have been. His tired mother invites Prietita in and offers her food. Prietita refuses politely, knowing that "they would offer a guest the last of their food and go hungry rather than appear bad-mannered." They tell her that they have crossed the river because the mother could not find work on the other side. However, here they have not found real work and are still doing odd jobs "in exchange for food and old clothes." Prietita offers to tell the neighbor women that Joaquin's mother is looking for work and urges him to bring wood the next day, but also to plan to play with her. As the days go by, Joaquin is less shy. Prietita always leaves him some of her lunch in a paper bag, but does not give it to him directly so as to "lessen his shame for being poor." She plans to take him to the herb woman when they know each other better.

One day, as they are playing a card game, a neighbor woman arrives shouting that the Border Patrol, la migra, *is looking for undocumented people. Joaquin is worried about his mother, and the two run to Joaquin's house. Prietita leads them to the herb woman, who hides the two Mexicans under the bed while the white patrolman and his Chicano partner question families on the block. No one admits to knowing any "illegals," although one woman points to the "gringo side of town," and everybody, even the Chicano* migra, *laughs. Luckily, no one stops at the herb woman's house. They all wait a while, then the herb woman (*curandera *in the accompanying Spanish text) serves them tea. She invites Prietita to gather herbs and tells her she will show her how to prepare a paste to heal Joaquin's arms. "'It's time for you to learn. You are ready now.'"*

COMMENT

The setting is in a section of Texas that was part of Mexico a hundred and fifty years ago. By accidents of birth and history, Prietita and Joaquin are citizens of different countries and members of different classes. However, they share a similar ethnic background and language. We can look at diversity within an ethnic group and at the ways different members respond to it. (Joaquin's Spanish is different from hers. How often have we heard people make fun of southern accents in English?) Some, like Prietita's cousin, make fun of the newcomers. Others, like the townspeople who refuse to give information to *la migra*, show solidarity. Prietita reaches out instinctively, as one human being to another. She notes the difference in class and language as interesting facts, not as divisions that will keep her from making a new friend. She appreciates the strengths of Joaquin and his mother. She helps as she is able, always respecting their pride and boundaries.

We can ask why people turn on each other for perceived differences and how we can find the strength to appreciate the differences and stand up to prejudice. We can look at the sources of strength, the traditions that sustain people, at the need for solidarity. We can explore issues of legal and illegal immigration, looking at immigration patterns and the way that diverse groups have been excluded or included in our country. For instance, when labor was needed to build the transcontinental railroad, Asians were encouraged to emigrate. Later, Asian immigration was blocked, only to be allowed within the past 30 years. Similarly, in times of boom economy, the border patrol looks the other way along the Rio Grande, but in times of recession, or when the harvests are over, control is tight. We can talk about our own immigrant backgrounds and how our people came to the United States (propelled by economic conditions in the homeland or abducted and enslaved). We can explore the prejudice that our own group encountered.

We can practice the skills of approaching everyone with an open mind and heart and of standing up to prejudice even when practiced by our own family members.

Book Talk

READ ALOUD

Previewing the book

Show the front and back covers and title page of the book and ask what students think the book will be about. Where do they think the action will take place? Read the short biographies of the author and illustrator. Locate South Texas on the map. Point out that Texas once belonged to Mexico. The Texans fought for independence (Remember the Alamo!) and the United States annexed Texas. However, the southern boundary was the Nueces River. After the Mexican-American War, it was the Rio Grande River. Has anyone

in the class been to South Texas? What is the climate like? What kinds of animals and
flowers are there?

Reading and responding to the book

Read the book through once, pausing only to explain possibly unfamiliar words (*mojados*,
mesquite, *la migra*, tarp, herb woman, *loteria*, *gringo*) and perhaps to ask what students think
will happen next, as when on p. 9 Prietita is debating what to do. Note that the book is
written in English and Spanish.

After you read the story, ask the students to pair up and talk about the book. What interests
them? What questions do they have? Encourage students to address each other as well as
the teacher. If there are Spanish speakers in the class, would they read part or all of the
book in Spanish?

Have students read other books about Mexico or South Texas? Have they read other books
about Spanish-speaking people in the United States? What were those books about? What
picture of Spanish-speaking people do they give? Do the students think that these pictures
are true? Elicit that there is enormous variety to the people who have Spanish-speaking
heritage. Remind the students that if Christopher Columbus's "encounter" had been
further North, all of us might speak Spanish.

Deepening students' understanding of the book

Read the author's statement on p. 2. Say that you will read the story again. Ask the
students to think about what the author might have seen when she was growing up that
would help her think of a story like this. Why did the author write the story? What are the
themes she is trying to convey? Elicit as many ideas as possible. Our emphasis here will be
on being open to people who are "different" and on standing against prejudice.

Say that you want them to think about what each character in the book is feeling and how
the characters change throughout the story. Ask them to look for foreshadowing. (For
example, Prietita thinks that she will take Joaquin to the herb woman for healing. We have
not met the herb woman, but she will play a pivotal role in helping Joaquin and his mother;
then she will affirm that Prietita is ready to learn to be a healer herself, presumably because
of the sensitivity and courage she has shown in the story.) Like the protagonist in *Your
Move*, Prietita comes to terms with herself and grows through her experiences.

Some possible stopping places include p.11 — what makes Prietita stop hesitating? What do
we think Tete is feeling? Tete's friends? Joaquin?

On p. 14, she sees that Joaquin and his mother are very poor from the place that they live in.
How does she respond to them? Does she make fun of them or respect them?

On p. 18, why can't they talk about the food? Why does she ask him to push her on the
swing?

When the immigration authorities come, Prietita doesn't hesitate to help Joaquin and his mother hide (pp. 22-23). What do we think she is feeling? What are Joaquin and his mother feeling?

Why does the herb woman say that Prietita is now ready to learn about healing (p. 30)?

NOTE: The art work in this book could lead to weeks of further study both of the natural world and of Mexican culture. Students could look at the symbolic elements in the homes of Joaquin and the herb woman. They could note the saying in Spanish on p. 15 that the broken blade can still fight. The class could take a field trip to a *botanica*. Students could learn about cacti and wildlife in Texas.

If anyone in the class is from Mexico or has relatives from Mexico or has traveled in Mexico, could they share aspects of Mexican culture with the class or invite an adult to speak? Are there simple recipes that the class can make?

How do Prietita and Joaquin change as the story develops?

There are two kinds of conflicts in the book: 1) interpersonal conflicts and 2) conflicts with government policies and practices. What are the interpersonal conflicts in the book, and what is the conflict with the government? Prietita is helping someone break the law, as are all of the people who say that they do not know if there are any "illegals." Do the students think Prietita is doing the right thing? Why? Why not?

Connecting the book to students' lives

Discussion: Ask the students, Can you remember a time when you saw someone being mistreated because they were "different"? Did anyone help the person who was being targeted? If so, what did that person do to help? Can you remember a time when <u>you</u> stood up for someone who was "different"? Call on a couple of volunteers to tell their stories. As with other discussions in the 4Rs curriculum that may raise strong emotions, students can be encouraged to take a few abdominal breaths together (see Unit 2) before and after each speaker. This is a way for students to calm themselves, and bring full awareness to their own emotions and those of their partner.

Writing: Write about a time when you saw someone being mistreated because they were different. Maybe that person was you! As she sees the boys calling Joaquin names, "Prietita felt her body go stiff." What is the author trying to tell us by describing this physical sensation? Do you recall any physical sensations when you saw another person being mistreated?

Did anyone stand up for the person being mistreated? If so, what did that person do to help? If no one helped, write about what you wish you or someone else would have done to help.

After Prietita and Joaquin become friends, she leaves food for him by the gate "to lessen his shame for being poor." This is an example of trying to take another's perspective – she is trying to be mindful of his need for food, and also of feelings he might have about accepting food from her. Write about a time where you tried to take someone else's perspective, or show empathy for another person (or, a time someone did this for you). What were your thoughts and feelings about this situation?

ROLE-PLAY

Ask for volunteers to role-play the scene of the boys teasing Joaquin. The teacher or a student teacher should play the part of Joaquin. Freeze the action just as someone picks up a rock. Ask the class for ideas about what different characters could do. What could friends of Tete do to stop the teasing? Is there anything that Joaquin could do? Act out different scenarios.

Applied Learning

Lesson 1

Objectives

Students will
- define culture and identify key aspects of culture
- name their own cultural background
- create culture banners with words and images that represent their cultures

Materials

- Agenda on chart paper or the chalkboard
- Construction paper and markers or crayons

Gathering: Attribute linking

Students stand in an area of the classroom where they can move around. When you call out a preference or attribute, those who have the preference or attribute in common find each other and stand together.

For example, if you call out, "Favorite season of the year," the students whose favorite season is spring will find each other and stand together, while students who prefer winter, fall, or summer will do the same.

Once the students are standing with others who share the same preference or attribute, you can ask each group to say something about why they're standing there or what it's like to be in that group: Would someone who likes spring give your reasons? How about those who like winter? And so on.

Continue with other attributes or preferences, such as favorite day of the week, favorite month of the year, favorite TV show, favorite sport. An interesting attribute is age order of children in the family (oldest, middle, youngest, only child), When the students are standing with others who have the same age order, you can ask each group, What's it like to be [oldest, youngest, etc.] What do you like about it? What's challenging?

Check agenda

Go over the objectives and the agenda.

Culture web

Write the word "culture" in the middle of a piece of chart paper. Ask the students to "free associate" with the word, sharing words or ideas that come to mind when they hear the word "culture."

Here's an example of how a "culture web" might begin to unfold:

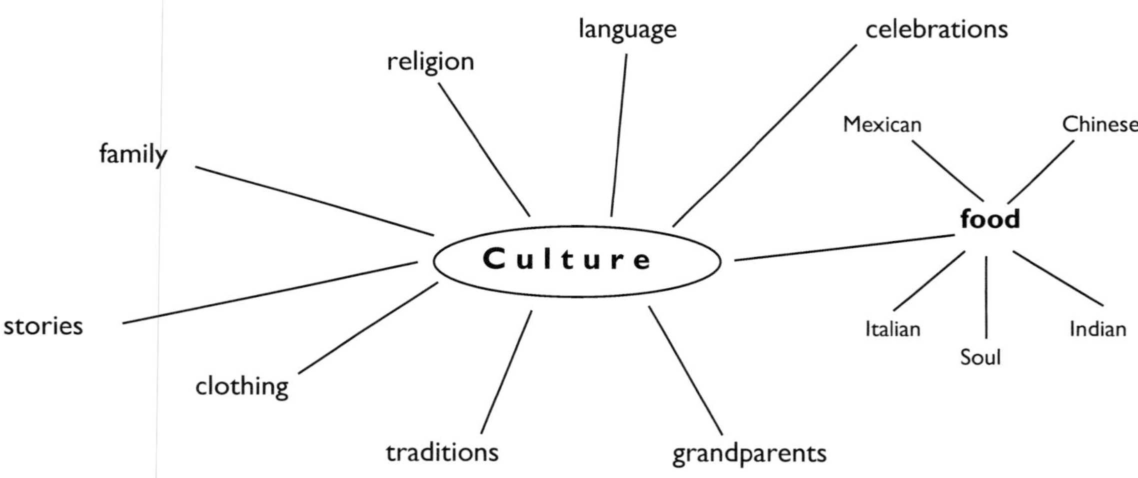

Ask, what is culture? Elicit the students' thinking. Help them develop a definition of culture as the particular values, beliefs, customs, and ways of life shared by a group of people.

Explain that the word "culture" is most commonly used in connection with ethnic groups, that is, groups defined by language, religion, or ancestry. Examples of ethnic groups in the United States are Native Americans, Italians, Irish, Japanese, African, Puerto Rican, Dominican, Mexican, German, Chinese, Caribbean, Arab, Southeast Asian, Korean, and many, many more. Ask, What ethnic groups do we have in our class? Ask for volunteers to name their ethnic backgrounds. If there is a world map in the room, show where our ancestors or we have come from.

Explain that in a complex modern society like the United States, there are other groups besides our ethnic group that we are part of and can choose to identify with. So while some people may identify most strongly with their ethnic backgrounds, others may identify most strongly with their work or occupation — for example, with being a teacher or a nurse. Another person might identify with their role in society (like being a parent or a student). Another might identify with being from a certain class background (like working class or middle class); still another, with being a feminist or a social activist or an artist. People in each of these groups share certain kinds of experiences, and may think of themselves as having certain values and life styles in common. Explain that in The 4Rs curriculum, we define culture broadly to include these kinds of groups as well as ethnic groups.

Culture banners

Explain that in this next activity, students will create banners to represent their cultural backgrounds. They will use crayons or markers to draw images and write words that say something about their culture.

To prepare students for making their banners, ask students to pair up and share with their partners their cultural background and the values that are important in their family. Model the activity by sharing about your own cultural background. Then call on a couple of volunteers to share their cultural backgrounds and a value important in their families.

Distribute construction paper and markers or crayons. Suggest that students write their family name in the middle of the paper and go on to add words and images that reflect their cultural background. While the students are doing their cultural banners, do one yourself.

Collect the students' banners and save them for the next session

Evaluation and closing

How was it for students to reflect on their cultural backgrounds? Send the talking piece around for students to share one word that names their feeling.

Lesson 2

Objectives
Students will
- share with the group the cultural banners they made in the previous session, and explain the meaning of the words and symbols on the banner

Materials
- Agenda on chart paper
- Talking piece
- Cultural banners the students created in the previous session

Gathering: Greetings

Ask students what a "greeting" is (saying hello, waving, etc.). Have them think for a minute about another gesture or movement they could use to greet someone. When everyone has an idea, ask one person to "greet" the person to their right using their gesture or movement; the person who is greeted should respond by mirroring that greeting. The second person then turns and greets the next person with the gesture or movement they thought of; this person responds by mirroring the second person's greeting, and so on around the circle.

The activity can also be done by having students move around the room, and exchange greetings with others that they meet. Continue until everyone has greeted 5-6 people.

Check agenda

Review the objectives and agenda for the lesson with the students.

Sharing cultural banners

With students seated in a circle (as usual), show them your cultural banner and explain the words and symbols. Describe a value that was important in your family.

Then pass the talking piece around for students to show the class their banners and explain the meaning of the words and symbols. Encourage them also to describe a value that's important in their family. How do they know that that value is important?

After each student makes a presentation about their banner, lead the class in applause.

Evaluation

Pass the talking piece around for students to share one thing they learned today about another person in the group.

Closing

Lead the students in a round of applause to celebrate the richness of diversity in their group.

Lesson 3

Objectives

Students will
- review the definitions of prejudice and discrimination and give examples
- review the definition of stereotypes
- explore an example—stereotypes of teenagers
- share examples of stereotypes of other groups

Materials

- Agenda on chart paper or the chalkboard
- A chart with the definitions of prejudice and discrimination, as follows:
  - Prejudice is a negative attitude or opinion not based on knowledge
  - Discrimination is action based on prejudice
- Chart paper (one piece for each of five or six student groups)
- Markers for each group

Gathering

Have the students pair up and tell each other about food they enjoy that comes from a culture different from their own.

Check agenda

Go over the objectives and the agenda.

Prejudice and discrimination

Explain that cultural differences can enrich our lives. The foods we enjoy from various cultures are just one of the ways we benefit from cultures different from our own. But unfortunately cultural differences are sometimes used as an excuse for mistreating people. We saw this in *Friends from the Other Side*. The boys called Joaquin names and were about to throw stones at him because he was "from the other side" of the border between the United States and Mexico.

Friends from the Other Side shows prejudice and discrimination and the pain they cause. Today we're going to review the meaning of those words.

Ask, what is prejudice? Elicit the students' thinking.

Referring to your chart with the definitions of prejudice and discrimination, explain that prejudice is a negative attitude or opinion that is not based on knowledge. To help us remember the definition, we might break the word into its roots: pre + judgment. We form an opinion about a person even before knowing the person. We pre-judge the person.

You might mention (or read them) the Dr. Suess book *Green Eggs and Ham*, which your students may be familiar with. The character in that story says again and again that he doesn't like green eggs and ham. Finally, when he tries them, he likes them. His original opinion was formed without knowledge. That's an example of prejudice.

Pete and his friends were prejudiced against *Joaquin*. Because they knew he came from Mexico, they had a negative attitude toward him without even knowing him. They assumed he wasn't as good as they were, and they used that as an excuse to mistreat him.

Ask whether the students can think of other examples of prejudice. Have they experienced prejudice directed at them? Have they ever had a negative attitude toward somebody at first, but then changed their mind when they got to know the person? Elicit examples from the students. Share an example from your own life if you think it would be helpful.

Again referring to your chart, explain that discrimination is doing something based on prejudice. If you are prejudiced toward certain kinds of people — if you have a negative attitude toward them because they are different from you in some way — and you do mean things to them, that's discrimination. *Pete and the boys were prejudiced against *Joaquin*, they acted on their prejudice, yelling at him and preparing to throw rocks at him.

Ask, What are other examples of discrimination — of someone doing mean or unfair things to another person who is different in some way? Elicit examples from several volunteers. Encourage the students to think of examples from their own lives.

Are prejudice and discrimination fair? What effect do they have on people? When things happen that are unfair, either to us or to someone else, what should we do? Ask the students to turn and talk with a partner for a couple of minutes to share their thoughts about those questions. After they're done talking in pairs, call on a couple of students to share their thoughts.

Introduce the students to the names for various kinds of mistreatment people experience because of differences. You might make a chart that lists target groups on the left and ask the students if they know the names for mistreatment of those groups. Fill in terms the students don't know. The completed chart might look like this:

Target Group	Systematic Mistreatment
Women	Sexism
people of color	Racism
Jewish people	anti-Semitism
Lesbian, gay, bisexual, transgender, and queer people	Homophobia
old people	Ageism
poor people	Classism
Muslims	Islamophobia

To help the students understand the chart, give them a couple of examples. If a girl wants to play basketball with a group of boys and the boys say, "No girls allowed. Go jump rope with the other girls," what kind of mistreatment would that be? If an African-American person gets turned down for buying a house and the house is sold to a white person with exactly the same qualifications, what kind of mistreatment would that be? How about Joaquin? The mistreatment he experienced is hard to classify. The boys felt free to discriminate against him because he was poor; he was from another country; he was in this country illegally. Are immigrants in our country experiencing discrimination today?

To wrap up this part of the lesson, leave the students with a question: How we can make our school and our classroom a place where everyone is treated with respect and no one is subjected to any kind of mistreatment.

First thoughts: Exploring stereotypes

Explain that one form prejudice takes is "stereotypes." Ask, What do we mean by "stereotype"? Elicit that a stereotype is a general statement about a group of people based on incomplete information.

Today we're going to explore stereotypes through an exercise called "First Thoughts." Have the students work in groups of four. Each group needs a piece of chart paper and markers. In their groups the students write the word "teenager" in the middle of the chart paper and draw a line around it. Then they fill the paper with their first thoughts about teenagers.

Explain that by "first thoughts" we mean what pops into our heads when we hear the word teenager. After giving it a little thought, we see immediately that our first thought doesn't apply to all teenagers. But still, the idea is in our heads.

Give the groups five or ten minutes to complete their "first thoughts" charts.   Then give each group a chance to share what they came up with. After all of the groups have presented, write "Teenagers" on the chalkboard, elicit from the class the main points that have emerged from their "first thoughts," and write them down. Your description might look something like this:

Teenagers

- like loud music
- are addicted to junk food
- are always on their phones
- are rowdy, rude, and disrespectful
- won't let anybody tell them what to do
- are totally into themselves

Discuss: The points above are generalizations or stereotypes about teenagers. Do some teenagers fit this description? Do all teenagers fit this description? Who can describe a teenager you know who is not like this? Is it fair to say or imply that all teenagers are like this?

What's the problem with stereotypes? Why is it a problem to say that a whole group of people (for example, teenagers) are rowdy and disrespectful, for example? What are the negative effects of stereotypes?

Can the students think of examples of stereotypes of other groups besides teenagers? Do the students think that Tete and the boys were willing to mistreat Joaquin because they had a stereotype in their minds of "people from the other side"? Have any of the students been mistreated by people who had a stereotype of their group?
Summarize by saying that stereotypes tend to create barriers that prevent people of different backgrounds from getting to know each other and being friends. We need to be aware of our stereotypes and stay open to people as individuals.

Evaluation

Ask students to pair up and talk with their partner about one thing they're taking away from today's lesson. After they've talked in pairs for a couple of minutes, call on a couple of volunteers to share their thoughts.

Closing

Give a high five to the person on your left to send high fives around the circle.

Lesson 4

Objectives

Students will
- understand the difference between "aggressive," "target," "bystander," and "ally" behaviors in situations where others are being treated unfairly
- increase their awareness of the responsibilities of bystanders to become allies
- generate ideas for standing up to unfair treatment directed at them or at others
- practice carrying out creative ideas in role-plays

Materials

- Agenda on chart paper or the chalkboard
- Handout, "Behavior in Bullying Situations"
- Handout, "How to Develop Role-plays"

Gathering

Turn off the lights and lead the students in five cycles of deep breathing (as introduced in Unit 2). Before starting the breathing, suggest that while breathing deeply students may want to travel in their minds to their peaceful place.

Check agenda

Go over the objectives and the agenda.

Four behaviors in bullying situations

Explain that in situations where people are being treated unfairly, there are often four kinds of behaviors happening at the same time. "Aggressive" behaviors are those that actively hurt others, either physically or emotionally. "Target" behaviors refer to things that the person being mistreated may do. "Bystander" behaviors are the things that people who are "standing by" or witnessing the mistreatment say or do. Although they are present, they are neither on the giving nor the receiving end of the mistreatment, and they may decide to try to stop unfair behaviors. "Ally" behaviors are efforts to stop the mistreatment and/or to support the person being targeted in some way.

In *Friends from the Other Side*, who was acting aggressively? Who was being targeted? Who was in the role of the bystander? Who acted as an ally? What qualities does Prietita have that enable her to stand up effectively for Joaquin and prevent the boys from attacking him?

What are other situations, either in literature, history, or their own lives, where people experienced mistreatment because they were different in some way? Who were those who acted aggressively? Who were those who were targeted? Who was in the bystander role? Who took on the role of ally? Ask the students to take out paper and pencil and jot down some quick thoughts.

After a couple of minutes, ask the students to share what they've written with a partner. Then give several volunteers a chance to share their thinking with the group.

What we can do

When we see someone being mistreated—being discriminated against or bullied—we have a choice. We can join the person doing the bullying. We can say to ourselves, "It's none of my business," and do nothing. Or we can try to help.

Ask, What do you think would be "The 4Rs choice"? What choice would Prietita want us to make?

Assuming we choose to try to help, what can we do? When we see someone being bullied or otherwise mistreated, what can we do to help? Prietita stopped the boys from throwing rocks at Joaquin, and she did other things, too. What did she do? Elicit students' ideas and ask them to back up their statements by referring to the text of the story. Record students' ideas on the chart labeled 'Things We Can Do."

Ask the students to pair up and share with their partners other ideas of things we can do to stop mistreatment and bullying if we see it happening in our school.

Give the students a couple of minutes to talk in pairs. Then call on each pair to share their ideas. Then add their ideas to the list of 'Things We Can Do."

The list might include the following:

- Confront the person doing the bullying and tell him or her to stop
- Get some friends together and ask the person doing the bullying to stop
- Make friends with the person who is being bullied
- Tell a teacher
- Tell a parent or guardian
- Tell the guidance counselor

Skits: Standing up against discrimination

Have the students work in groups of four or five. In each group, students begin with a go-round in which each student shares a time they were treated unfairly or watched someone else be treated unfairly. Then the group chooses one of the situations described in the go-round to develop as a skit. The skit should portray an incident in which someone is mistreated because they are different and either the person being target or a bystander or both stand up and stop the mistreatment. Encourage the students to use their skills in listening and assertiveness to come up with effective responses.

Each group presents its skit, followed by a brief discussion: Have others in the class either experienced or witnessed an incident like this? What strategy for stopping the mistreatment did the skit show us? Were 4Rs skills involved in the strategy? Do you think the approach presented in the skit would work in the real world? Why? Why not? Could you see yourself actually using that approach?

Closing: Balancing in Pairs

This is a variation on the Balancing activity (Unit 5, Lesson 3)

Have students find a partner and create a balanced position involving both people. Partners may support and steady each other by holding hands, leaning against each other's shoulders, balancing back to back, touching knees, etc.

Ask for a few volunteers to demonstrate their balanced position.

What is the connection between this activity, and "standing up" for another person?

Additional Activities

Make time for silence

During this time the lights are off. No writing, drawing, reading, no gadgets. Just sitting. Encourage students to put their hands on their knees. Students can close their eyes if they want. You can tell them that they can let their minds use the silence as they wish. Or you can suggest ways they might use the silence. For example, they could

- practice abdominal breathing (introduced in Unit 2)
- pay attention to their breathing

- take themselves to a peaceful place in their mind
- recall a time they had fun
- recall something they like to do

After the time of silence, ask for a couple of volunteers to share where their minds went during the time. Make time for silence every day, preferably at the same time, such as after lunch or recess or as the first and last actions of the day.

By giving students the opportunity to experience time for silence on a daily basis, you'll be instilling a habit that will serve them well for the rest of their lives.

Consider having your students keep a 4Rs journal

Writing (drawing for younger students) is an excellent way to reinforce and consolidate learning. A journal enables students to put all of their Book Talk writing in one place. You can also give them a few minutes after each 4Rs lesson to jot down a few thoughts about what they're taking away or how they're planning to use what they've just learned. If a student tries a new skill, s/he might want to write about what happened. Did it bring a positive result? If a student is stuck in a conflict with someone, s/he might want to do some writing to sort it out and imagine some solutions. You can give them standard journals and encourage them to decorate them.

By having students keep journals, you will be introducing them to a habit or practice that can serve them well the rest of their lives.

Class meetings for problem solving

In this kind of class meeting the teacher empowers students, facilitating a process by which students apply the skills they're developing through 4Rs lessons to real-life situations in the classroom and the school. By now, your students should have the foundational skills (managing feelings, listening, assertiveness) to be good problem solvers. Also, Unit 5 has introduced the ABCDE problem-solving model, an approach young people can grasp easily. A free downloadable copy of Morningside Center's comprehensive guide *Class Meetings for Problem Solving* is available by request.

Related Books

America Is her Name by Luis J. Rodriguez, illus. Carlos Vasquez

Annie's Promise by Sonia Levitan

The Canning Season by Margaret Carlson, illustrated by Kimanne Smith (example of memoir)

Freak the Mighty by W. R. Philbrick, Rodman Philbrick (move is called "The Mighty")

Just Like Home/Como En Mi Tierra by Elizabeth I. Miller, illus. Mora Reisberg, trans. Teresa Mlawer

Prietita and the Ghost Woman/Prietita y la Llorena by Gloria Anzaldua, illus. Christina Gonzalez. Bilingual

The Woman Who Outshone the Sun: The Legend of Lucia Zenteno, Rosaluna Zubizarreta, Harriet Rohmer, David Schecter, Alejandro Cruz Martinez, illus. Fernando Olivera. Bilingual

My Name Is Bilal by Asma Mobin-Uddin

For teachers who want more activities for celebrating diversity and countering discrimination, a great book is *Open Minds to Equality: A Sourcebook of Learning Activities to Affirm Diversity and Promote Equity*, 3rd Edition, by Nancy Schniedewind and Ellen Davidson.

Handout 1 • Unit 6

Behavior in the Bullying Situations

Aggressive Behavior

This is behavior aimed at hurting others, either physically or emotionally.

Target Behaviors

Target behavior refers to the ways the person being targeted responds to being targeted—what they feel, what they do.

Bystander Behaviors

When bullying occurs, there are often people standing by and watching it happen. These are "bystanders." They didn't start the aggressive behavior and they aren't being targeted for mistreatment. Bystander behavior may include the following:

- watching without doing anything
- encouraging the aggressive behavior
- stirring up trouble behind the scenes
- helping the person being targeted (see below).

Ally Behaviors

Ally behaviors aim to help the person being mistreated. These behaviors may include the following:

- helping the person being targeted while the mistreatment is occurring
- offering help afterward
- making friends with the target in order to keep the target from being alone and more vulnerable
- going with the target to tell an adult
- reporting the mistreatment to a trusted adult.

How to Develop Role-plays

1. Each student describes a bullying situation the student has seen, heard about, or participated in.

2. The group chooses one story or incident from which to create a skit.

3. The person whose story it is becomes the director of the skit, assigning parts to the various members of the group.

4. The actors play the situation and freeze the action at the point where the person acting aggressively is harming the person begin targeted.

5. If the skit is to show a person being targeted standing up for her- or himself, the group discusses an effective approach that a person being targeted might take. If the skit is to show ally behavior, the group discusses an effective approach that an ally might take.

6. The group decides on an effective strategy and rehearses this strategy. The skit is now ready to be seen by the whole class.

7. To announce the presentation of a skit, the whole class says, "One, two, three, action!"

8. When the skit is over, everybody applauds.

5

Unit 7 Theme

Making a Difference

Unit 7 Book Selection

Sweet Clara and the Freedom Quilt by Deborah Hopkinson
Dragonfly Books, Alfred A. Knopf, New York, 1995

Activities

- Our Year with The 4Rs
- A Gift I Can Give to the World [Making a Pledge]
- Completing and Presenting our Pledges
- Additional Activities

Introduction

In this unit we will look at stories of individuals who, working with others, acted courageously to make the world a better place. Across the grades some of the characters are fictional and some are real people. What they have in common is the understanding that we are linked together in our struggles for peace, freedom, and justice.

In each story at each grade level there is an individual who channels his or her fear and anger at injustice to constructive action. That action makes a difference in the lives of others.

The stories of these outstanding individuals are inspiring, but we do not have to be heroes to make a difference. Whenever we help a neighbor, intervene to keep a quarrel from escalating, refuse to rise to the bait of anger, teach someone something useful, give a heartfelt compliment, we are building community and making a difference. Each act may seem isolated, but each builds on others to empower us to act courageously and create peaceful, just communities.

Since this is the last unit of the curriculum, students will reflect on their year with The 4Rs: the stories they've heard, the games they've played, the skills they've learned. The 4Rs teaches leadership skills that will help them make a contribution to the communities they become part of — from the classroom to the world.

In this unit students will also reflect on times they have made a difference for others and identify the strengths they have that enabled them to do so. They will think of something concrete they can do in the here and now to make the world a better place and make a pledge to do it. As they share their pledges with the class, their classmates will let them know that they have the support of their 4Rs friends behind them.

In this unit

	Ideas	Skills
Literacy	• Words and pictures can tell a story • Stories can show us ways to act in our own lives • Stories have characters • Stories may be told through poetry • Some poems are prose poems	• Summarizing the action • Identifying the main idea • Providing evidence to back up one's assertions • Identifying the personal qualities of characters in a story • Making connections between stories and our lives
Social and Emotional Learning	• We can work together to make the world safer and fairer • Everyone can do something to make a difference • It takes courage to stand up for what we believe	• Reflecting on past experience and drawing conclusions • Identifying our strengths • Generating ideas • Planning a course of action to make a difference • Making a pledge

Sweet Clara and the Freedom Quilt, by Deborah Hopkinson, paintings by James Ransome. Dragonfly Books, Alfred A. Knopf, New York, 1995.

SUMMARY

Young Clara, an enslaved child, has been taken from her mother to work in the fields of Home Plantation. She is inconsolable, but finds strength in the thought that someday she will rejoin her mother (although privately she admits that she wouldn't know how to find her way back). " 'Well, you better start eatin' all you can, Sweet Clara,' " says her field mate, Jack, " 'Or else you won't make it.' " Indeed, Aunt Rachel, the woman who cares for Clara, is afraid that Clara will never survive the rough work of the fields and vows to find a way to bring Clara up to the Big House, where the work is not as brutal. She brings home scraps of material for Clara to learn to be a seamstress. The mistress's daughter will be married in the spring, and Rachel hopes to persuade her to use Clara as an extra seamstress.

The plan works, for Clara has an aptitude for sewing. While she is in the Big House, she hears travelers who talk to the cook. Several slaves have run away, and the owners are concerned about the success of the Underground Railroad. The men Clara overhears say that more slaves would take advantage of the Railroad if they had a map. Later, Clara asks Aunt Rachel to explain about the railroad. Aunt Rachel shows her the North Star and describes the purpose of a map. Clara draws the beginnings of a map in the dirt, but wonders "how could I make a map that wouldn't be washed away by the rain — a map that would show the way to freedom?" Then one day, as she is sewing a patch on a blue blanket, she realizes that the patch looks like the cow pond and the stitches like footprints around it. From that day forward she saves every scrap of material she can and vows to make a map in quilt form.

Soon, the quarters are abuzz. Someone has escaped. It's Jack, but after five days they find him. When Clara goes to see him on Sunday, he "didn't smile the way he used to." She starts to draw in the dirt what she has figured out. Jack doesn't pay attention at first, then he realizes what she's doing and he fills in more information from what he learned while running. Months go by as Clara works on the quilt, often having to wait a long time for the right kind of cloth. "The quilt got bigger and bigger, and if folks knew what I was doin', no one said. But they came by the sewin' room to pass the time of day whenever they could." And in passing the time of day, they conveyed information: Mr. Morse's house is " ' twenty miles north of here' "; " 'they gon' plant corn in the three west fields on the Verona plantation this year' "; the swamp next to Home Plantation is "'a nasty place. But listen up, Clara, and I'll tell you how I thread my way in and out of there as smooth as yo' needle in that cloth.' "

Finally, the quilt is finished. Aunt Rachel fingers it lightly, touching the boat next to the Ohio River that can take people to freedom. She tries to sound cheerful as she suggests that Clara use the quilt after she marries young Jack. But Clara knows that she wants to leave it behind, for others to use. She and Jack escape during a three-day rain, returning to Clara's birthplace for her mother, who now has another child. Eventually they all reach the Ohio River. Along the way, Clara sees all "the things people told me about, all the tiny stitches I took, now I could see real things."

They make it to Canada, and Clara remembers the night they left, when Aunt Rachel asked Clara to cover her with the quilt: " 'I'm too old to walk, but not too old to dream. And maybe I can help others follow the quilt to freedom.' "Indeed, Clara tells the reader, "Aunt Rachel kept her word." She knows that people come to look at the quilt "because some of them come and tell me how they used it to get free. But not all are as lucky as we were, and most never can come." Still, Clara longs for a quilt "that would spread over the whole land, and the people just follow the stitches to freedom, as easy as taking a Sunday walk."

COMMENT

This multi-layered story with the beautiful pictures and happy ending offers myriad opportunities to uncover the lives of the enslaved Africans. Neither author nor illustrator shows us the horror of slavery in graphic detail, but the understatements speak volumes and the pictures reveal undying resistance. First, as Clara is torn from her mother, we see how slavery destroyed families. With Aunt Rachel, we see the way a community of people cared for those who were not blood kin. Rachel fears that Clara cannot survive in the fields, but she knows that she cannot appeal to her mistress except through self-interest. Therefore, she teaches Clara her skills and thereby saves her life. We can guess that Jack has also helped her learn what to do in the fields. When Jack runs away, we are not told what happens to him, only that after being caught, he "didn't smile the way he used to."

Slowly, as Clara's dream takes shape in the form of the quilt, others rally to help her. No one ever says it out loud, but they all know what she is doing. And she is doing it under the noses of the masters. This is an opportunity to look at other forms of resistance. There were, of course, revolts, which were brutally suppressed. There was the Underground Railroad, which can be examined in depth as a network of resistance by enslaved Africans, freed Africans, and religious and secular people of European heritage. And then there was the daily resistance, the myriad ways in which enslaved people claimed their humanity in the midst of barbarism: Jack helping Clara, Rachel thinking of Clara's future, Clara creating something for others, the passers-by who give Clara information, Cook, who cares for the men who toil for the visitors to the Big House. In Julius Lester's book *Long Journey Home* there is an essay about the ways in which people resisted by only doing a certain amount of work when they could get away with it, spitting in the food they prepared for the owners, sabotaging property if they could. Further exploration could take us to the black church, which provided and still provides a network of services and a bedrock of strength.

We can compare Clara's quilt to *The Keeping Quilt*. They served different purposes, but both linked their owners to a community that was searching for freedom and yet retained its roots.

There are opportunities for creative work with quilts, for mapping, for historical research, for role-playing.

Book Talk

READ ALOUD

Previewing the book

Show the front and the back covers and title page of the book and ask what students think the book will be about. Where do they think the action takes place? What do they notice about each picture? What do they think is shown in the picture? Read the dedications and ask if everyone knows what a plantation is. Note that the illustrator is the same one who illustrated *Your Move*. Note that he seems to have had an ancestor who was enslaved on one of the plantations that will be mentioned in the book. Ask students what they notice about the illustrations for each book. (Does *Your Move* have a more modern feel to it than *Sweet Clara*?)

Reading and responding to the book

Read the book through once, pausing only to ask students if they can guess what Clara is planning. Students may notice that the book is written to approximate Southern speech patterns. It's not necessary to go into linguistics, but it might be interesting to point out that almost all the books we read could easily be written phonetically to approximate the speech pattern of the region in which the action takes place. (Harry Potter, after all, would have an English accent, and in fact the American editions of the first books contain words that have been changed to American rather than British English. Books about the American West used to be written with western accents but rarely are today. The characters in *Little Women* would certainly have New England accents.) Here the author is trying to bring the reader into the mind of a twelve-year-old girl as well as into her time period through the use of language.

You may also want to point out that sewing machines were not yet used in the home, and all clothing and household furnishings such as sheets and drapes were made at home or by seamstresses or tailors.

After you read the story, ask the students to pair up and talk about the book. What interests them? What questions do they have? Encourage students to address each other as well as the teacher.

Have students read other books about slavery or the Underground Railroad? What do the students know about the experience of enslaved Africans, about the resistance to slavery? What movies or television shows have the students seen? What images do they have?

The issue of slavery is a painful one that affects every person in the United States, regardless of when or how their ancestors arrived or whether or not their ancestors were directly involved. Talking about slavery is likely to bring up strong feelings, and teachers should allow time for students to share and discuss feelings that arise.

Deepening students' understanding of the book

Read through the story again, asking the students to note how the characters watch out for each other and help each other. They may make a connection to the way that the characters helped each other in *Brothers in Hope* (Unit 5).   Ask them to think about how they would feel if they were a character in this book. How would they survive the backbreaking labor, the separation from loved ones?

Ask them to think about why the author wrote this book. Given what they know from other books, what does the author want to express? (The author understates the extremely oppressive conditions under which the characters live and focuses on their survival and resistance. Our emphasis here is also on the everyday courage of people working together in even the worst of circumstances to bring about change.)

Ask them to look at the way that Clara changes and grows as the book progresses. She is depressed and bereft at the beginning, (p.2), but still defiant. Slowly she learns about the outside world, the Big House, Canada, the possibility of freedom, (pp. 8-13). She learns patience (p. 20). She has courage, but she waits until she has knowledge to act on her plan.

Ask the students to notice what isn't said in the book. How does Clara's mother feel? What happened to Jack when he ran away? Why is he willing to try again? Are Jack and Clara in love? What is Rachel feeling as she sees Clara prepare the quilt? (Is it possible that Rachel had children who were sold away from her?) Do other slaves want to escape also? Are many others afraid to try for good reasons? What phrases and scenes help us guess the answers to these questions?

Notice the foreshadowing of the map (" 'Truth was, I'd be lost before I got through the fields. . . .But I didn't give up dreamin'.' "), p. 2; "I liked to piece the scraps together to make pretty patterns of colors," p. 4; " 'It be easy if you could get a map' ", p. 11). Notice the descriptive language: "I listened so hard it felt like my ears must be growing right out of my head and gettin' big with listening." (p. 11); "I began to squirrel away these bits of cloth. . . .I started piecin' the scraps of cloth with the scraps of things I was learnin' " (p. 17); " 'But listen up, Clara, and I'll tell you how I thread my way in and out of there as smooth as yo' needle in that cloth.' " (p. 20); "It was like being in a dream you already dreamed" (p. 24).

Chart the steps that Clara takes to gain her freedom: setting a goal; gathering information; making a plan; using help from others; enlisting an ally (Jack); waiting for the right time to leave (under cover of a storm); following the plan while still being flexible (she wasn't prepared to find a baby when she found her mother, but they were able to still go ahead with the plan).

Connecting the book to students' lives

Discussion: Clara's goal was to escape to the North and gain her freedom. Ask the students to pair up and talk about a goal they have. It can be a big goal like Clara's or something smaller, like making a friend or getting better at a sport. If some students don't have goal, this is an opportunity for them to think of a goal they'd like to have. Are they going to middle school next year? Do they have a goal for next year in middle school.

After the students talk in pairs, send the talking piece around for students to share a goal they have or a goal they would like to have. Why is this goal important to them? Are they taking steps to achieve it?

Writing: Ask the students to write about the goal, including what they shared with their partner and in the go round.

Before going to the Big House for the first time, Clara says, "Next morning I tried to eat some corn bread, but my insides was all knotted up." (p. 5) What does this physical sensation suggest about the emotions she was experiencing? Write about a time when you were about to have a new experience, and any physical sensations you recall.

ROLE-PLAY

Ask students to split up into groups of four and prepare scenes from the book to present to the class.

Applied Learning

Lesson 1

Objectives

Students will
- recall the books they've read, the games they've played, and they skills they've practiced in The 4Rs
- identify their favorite and most memorable experiences with The 4rs
- identify important things they have learned from The 4Rs.

Materials

- Agenda on chart paper or the chalkboard
- Talking piece
- Chart paper, masking tape, markers
- Copy of the handout "Overview of The 4Rs" (attached)

Group Balancing

This is a variation on the "Balancing in Pairs" activity (Unit 6, Lesson 4). Ask students to work in groups of 3-4 to create a balanced position that involves everyone in the group.

Each person should be balancing, and each person should be connected to and supporting another person in keeping their balance.

Ask for a few volunteers to demonstrate their balanced group shape.

Would it be possible to hold this position without the support of others in the group? What does this activity have to do with the story of Clara and the freedom quilt? With the theme of "Making a Difference"?

Check agenda

Tell the students that in this lesson they're going to take some time to think about their work this year with The 4Rs. They'll recall The 4Rs stories, the games, and the skills.

Our Year with The 4Rs

Clara had a goal of gaining her freedom and reuniting with her mother. Point out that as a class we have had a goal this year. In Unit 1 of The 4Rs we set the goal a creating a caring classroom community where all of us would try hard to use put-ups and never put each other down. Have we done that? Have we accomplished that goal? Thumbs up if you think we've done a pretty good job of putting each other up. Call on a couple of students to share their thoughts.

After we set our goal, we read stories and learned skills to help us make our vision real in the classroom. What are some of the stories we read in The 4Rs? Call on several volunteers to say book titles and characters they remember.

What are some of the skills we practiced? Call on several volunteers to name some of the skills and recall some of the activities we used to practice them.

Distribute copies of the handout "Overview of The 4Rs." Referring to the handout, briefly remind the students of the themes of the seven 4Rs units and the primary skill introduced and practiced in each unit.

Ask students to pair up and share with their partner their favorite 4Rs story. What did they like about it?

With the students now back in a circle, send the talking piece around for students to share their favorite story and why they liked it.

Now ask students to pair up again and share a skill they practiced in The 4Rs that they have found useful. How has it been useful? Have they used it outside of school? How?

Send the talking piece around for students to name 4Rs skills that have made a difference for them. Have they used any of the skills outside of the classroom? If so, ask that they tell the story of their doing that.

Evaluation

What's one thing you learned from The 4Rs that you most want to remember if you forget everything else? Depending on how much time is left, pass the talking piece around, inviting everyone to speak, or have students share with partner, then ask a couple of volunteers to share with the group.

Closing

"Rhythm": Students close their eyes and begin to clap in whatever way they want. Have them continue until you call time. In most cases, the cacophony gradually evolves into a discernable rhythm, which demonstrates a natural human tendency toward order and cooperation.

Lesson 2

Objectives

Students will
- recall the gift Clara made to help others escape slavery
- identify a gift they can give to the world
- make a pledge to give the gift

Materials

- Hugg-A-Planet for use as a talking piece
- Agenda on chart paper or the chalkboard
- Chart paper for recording students' ideas
- Copies of the handout "My Gift for the World" for all students.

Gathering

Students say their names preceded by a positive adjective that starts with the same letter as their name. For example, Dynamic Deanna.

Check agenda

Go over the objectives and the agenda.

A gift I can give to the world

Clara's freedom quilt was a gift she created to help herself and other slaves escape to freedom. The quilt was a gift she gave to the world. Note that we usually think of gifts as things you buy in a store. But gifts can also be ways you help other people. By helping slaves to freedom, Clara gave them something much more precious than anything they could buy in a store.

Explain that you're going to give students the opportunity to think of gifts they'd like to give to the world. It could be taking some action, however small, to change something that's unfair. Or they might think about their families, their friends, people they know, people they've read about. How can students contribute to the happiness of these people? How can students make a difference in their lives? The gift should be something concrete — something a student could actually do. To help the students understand, give an example from your own life.

Give students a minute or two in silence to think about what their gift to the world might be. They can write or sketch some ideas, if that is helpful.

Ask students to pair up and share with their partners some ideas for ways they might make a positive difference for others — gifts they can give to the world. Emphasize once again that they think of concrete things — things they could actually do here and now — not something huge and far away like "world peace."

Using the Hugg-A-Planet as a talking piece, invite the students to share their ideas of gifts they might give to the world.

When the students have finished sharing their ideas, say that they are going forth with a year of 4Rs work under their belts. They have many skills and gifts they can give to others. They have thought of some ideas. Now you'd like them to choose one that they'll actually promise to do. You're going to ask them to make a *pledge*.

Ask if they know what a pledge is. Remind them that every morning in most public schools, children recite The Pledge of Allegiance. Ask them if they understand what they're doing when they recite that pledge. What's the meaning of it? Elicit that in reciting the Pledge people are making a promise. That's what a pledge is — it's a promise. In reciting the pledge people are promising to be loyal to our country, the United States, and to its values of liberty and justice.

NOTE: The Pledge of Allegiance was written by a Baptist minister named Francis Bellamy, and first published in 1892 in a popular children's magazine, "The Youth's Companion." It was adopted by Congress as the official national pledge in 1942. The words, "under God," were added in 1954.

Explain that today you want the students to begin work on personal pledges to contribute to the lives of others. They'll be choosing one of the ideas they came up with and promising to do it.

Pass out copies of the handout "My Gift for the World" for students to begin drafting their pledges. Explain that first they'll do a draft. Then they'll revise it, making sure it says clearly what they plan to do and uses correct spelling, etc. When they have completed a good draft, they can copy the pledge on a fresh copy of the handout, and illustrate their pledge.

Model this activity by writing your own pledge before circulating in the classroom to help students decide on a specific thing they will do and to help them with writing and revising.

Once they're happy with their revised draft, give them a fresh pledge sheet and colored markers, pencils, or crayons so that they can begin creating the final version. It's unlikely that they'll finish their pledges in this lesson. They'll have time in the next lesson to finish up.

Evaluation

Pass the Hugg-A-Planet around for students to share one word that names how they're feeling about pledging (promising) to give a gift to the world.

Closing: Tree in a Storm

Ask students if they have ever seen a tree standing in a storm or a strong wind. What parts of the tree moves in a storm? (Branches, leaves) What parts of the tree don't move? (Trunk, roots)

Have students stand in a position with their feet firmly planted on the floor, like the roots of a tree. Have them notice the space around them, and where others are standing. Ask them to imagine that they are a tree in an approaching storm and to move their bodies like a tree as the wind gets stronger. (Some students may want to close their eyes to imagine this). Say: "At first there is just a gentle breeze blowing the leaves and small branches….Now the wind is getting stronger, and some of the larger branches are moving as well….Now the storm is here – there is rain and strong winds moving the whole upper part of the tree, but the roots are holding firm….The storm is starting to pass and the wind is slowing down….And now the storm has passed and the wind is blowing softly until….it is still."

Ask for a few volunteers to describe what this was like. Ask, How was Clara like a tree in a storm? How can making a pledge help you to stand firmly, like a tree in a storm, when you try to make change happen in your life?

Lesson 3

Objectives

Students will
- complete their pledges
- identify a quality they'll need in order to carry it out
- receive a symbolic gesture of support from the group

Materials

- Copies of the handout "My Gift for the World"
- Markers for writing and drawing

- Hugg-A-Planet as a talking piece

Gathering

Pass the talking piece around for students to appreciate someone in the class or in their life beyond the classroom who has helped them—someone they're grateful for.

Check agenda

Go over the objectives and the agenda.

Completing our pledges

Hand out the drafts of pledges that the students worked on during the last session. Say that during this session they will complete the pledges and share them with the group. If some students have pledges too private to share, they can talk about what it was like for them to create this pledge. Ask whether anyone has questions.

Hand out the drafts and fresh copies of the handout "My Gift for the World" as needed, and give students time to complete a good copy of the pledge they are making.

Ask students to share their pledges in pairs. In addition to describing their pledge to their partner, ask them to think of a personal quality or resource they might need to carry out their pledge. Give them some examples. If they are pledging to help a younger sibling learn to ride a bike, they might need *patience*. If they're going to help a parent with a project around the house, they might need *time*. If they're going to ask grocery store owners to contribute food for a food pantry, they might need *courage*.

Presenting our pledges and getting support from the group

Bring students back in a circle to hold up their pledges and describe the gift they're planning to give to the world. When each student is done, s/he names a personal quality or resource s/he will need to carry out the pledge.

After the student names the quality or resource, lead the students in making a symbolic gesture of support as follows: You and the students stand and direct your attention to the student who has just named the quality or resource s/he will need. Lead the students in raising their arms high up over their heads. Together you and the students bring your arms down pointing toward the student and saying in unison, "We give you ________!" (Name whatever quality or resource the student says s/he will need. Following the examples above, the group might say "We give you patience!" or "We give you time!" or "We give you courage!"

After each student has spoken, close the activity by inviting the group to close their eyes and take five deep abdominal breaths together. Ask them to imagine that they are breathing in all the gifts to the world, as well as all the personal qualities that have been named.

Closing

"Today's closing activity will celebrate our work together this year and the fun we had and the things we learned through The 4Rs."

Ask the students to stand in a circle and hold hands. "We'll start by bending over together, holding hands. Slowly we'll begin raise up and then quickly lift our arms high up over our heads. As we do that, we're all going to say

Yeeeeeeeeeeeeeeeeeeeeeeeeeeeeeeessssssssssssssssssssssssssssssssss!

Lead the students in this gesture to wrap up their year with a powerful YES!

Additional Activities

Turning anger into action for justice

When Clara is taken from her mother to work in the fields of the Home Planation, she is inconsolable. Clara channeled the outrage at the injustice done her into a patient, steady determination to escape from the plantation, find her mother, and get to freedom.

Like Clara, many people have channeled their anger into the struggle for justice. With your students, generate a list of people who were angry about some injustice and decided to do something about it. The list might include: Frederick Douglass, Rosa Parks, Martin Luther King, Jr., Jane Addams, Susan B. Anthony, Ralph Nader, Rachel Carson, Mother Jones, Malcolm X, Mohandas Gandhi, Cesar Chavez, Dolores Huerta.

Have each student pick a person from the list to research and report on. To make this a cooperative activity, have the students work in pairs or small groups to choose a person, write a report, and prepare a presentation for the class.

Map Making

To make her quilt an accurate map, Clara had to listen to the stories of others with deep attention and awareness. Ask the students to make a map of their classroom, school, or the neighborhood immediately around the school (the latter may involve taking a walk around the neighborhood, paying close attention to details). How does creating a map help you to become more mindful of and attentive to your surroundings?

Related Books

The Keeping Quilt treats the quilt theme as do most quilt books, focusing on tradition, family, continuity. There are opportunities for research into quilting and its role in both the United States and in Africa. Faith Ringgold has created many story quilts telling both her own family stories and stories from African-American history. A true story of a folk artist who was born into slavery is in *Stitching Stars: The Story Quilts of Harriet Powers*, by Mary E. Lyons. Powers, who could not read or write, but who was deeply religious, created a story quilt of the Bible that now hangs in the Smithsonian Museum. A Civil-War era book with a quilt theme is *Selina and the Bear Paw Quilt*, by Barbara Smucker, illustrated by Janet Wilson. It follows the life of a Mennonite family that flees to Canada to escape persecution for their pacifist beliefs during the war.

Jacqueline Woodson, whose many books are read in classrooms, has also written a quilt book called *Show Way*. Like Patricia Polacco, she traces the story of her family, in this case through a quilt created by an enslaved ancestor. The art on each page is a veritable encyclopedia of knowledge about the era it covers and would be worth reports by students.

In addition, there are several books at various reading levels about the Underground Railroad and the Civil War. Among them are

Aunt Harriet's Underground Railroad in the Sky by Faith Ringgold
Barefoot: Escape on the Underground Railroad by Pamela Duncan Edwards
The Butterfly by Patricia Polacco
The Drinking Gourd: A Story of the Underground Railroad by F.N. Manjo, illustrated by Fred Brenner.
Follow the Drinking Gourd by Bernardine Connolly, Yvonne Buchanan, illus.
Follow the Drinking Gourd by Jeanette Winter
Freedom Train by Dorothy Sterling (biography of Harriet Tubman)
If You Traveled on the Underground Railroad by Ellen Levine, Larry Johnson, illus.
A Knock at the Door by Eric Sonderling, illustrated by Wendy Wassink Ackison
Open Minds to Equality: A Sourcebook of Learning Activities to Affirm Diversity and Promote Equity, 3rd edition, by Nancy Schniedewind and Ellen Davidson.
Pink and Say by Patricia Polacco (two young Civil War soldiers)
Sisters Against Slavery: A Story About Sarah and Angelina Grimke by Stephanie Sammartino McPherson, illustrated by Karen Ritz
To Be a Slave, by Julius Lester, illustrated by Tom Feelings, uses narratives from ex-slaves to describe life during slavery. The essays in the 30th anniversary edition describe the author's motivation and experiences since the book first appeared. Lester deals with the same material in a work of fiction for advanced young readers called *Long Journey Home*.
True North: A Novel of the Underground Railroad by Kathryn Lasky
The Underground Railroad by Raymond Bial (nonfiction reference)

Handout 1 ◆ Unit 7

Overview of The 4Rs™ for Grade 5

	Theme	Story
Unit 1	Building Community: Creating a Vision	The Keeping Quilt
Unit 2	Feelings	The Mysterious Traveler
Unit 3	Listening	Encounter
Unit 4	Assertiveness	Your Move
Unit 5	Problem Solving	Brothers in Hope
Unit 6	Diversity / Countering Bullying	Friends from the Other Side
Unit 7	Making a Difference	Sweet Clara and the Freedom Quilt

My Gift for the World

Name_________________________________ **Class**__________ **Date**______________

School____

City______________________________________ **State**_________________________________

I pledge to ____

____

____

Here's what it might look like

Bibliography

Works cited in The 4Rs: activities adapted from or permission given for use.

Derman-Sparks, Louise, *Anti-Bias Curriculum: Tools for Empowering Young Children*. National Association for the Education of Young Children, Washington, D.C. 1989.

Kreidler, William J., *Conflict Resolution in the Middle School: A Curriculum and Teacher's Guide*. esr / Educators for Social Responsibility, Cambridge, MA. 1994.

Kreidler, William J., *Creative Conflict Resolution: More Than 200 Activities for Keeping Peace in the Classroom K-6*. Good Year Books / Scott, Foresman and Company, Glenview, Illinois. 1984.

Kreidler, William J., *Elementary Perspectives: A Teaching Guide to Concepts of Peace*. ESR, Cambridge, MA. 1990.

Kreidler, William J., *Teaching Conflict Resolution Through Children's Literature, Grades K-2*. Scholastic Professional Books, New York. 1994.

Kreidler, William J. and Lisa Furlong, *Adventures in Peacemaking: A Conflict Resolution Activity Guide for School-age Programs*. Project Adventure. 1995.

Kreidler, William J. and Sandy Tsubokawa Whittall, *Early Childhood Adventures in Peacemaking*, 2nd edition. ESR, Cambridge, MA. 1999.

Prutzman, Priscilla et al., *The Friendly Classroom for a Small Planet*. New Society Publishers, Gabriola Island, BC, Canada, 1988. © Children's Creative Response to Conflict, P.O. Box 271, Nyack, NY 10960. Tel. (845) 353-1796.

Ray, Peggy and Sheila Alson, Linda Lantieri, and Tom Roderick, *Resolving Conflict Creatively: A Teaching Guide for Grades Kindergarten Through Six*. Board of Education of the City of New York, New York. 1993, 1996.

Schneidewind, Nancy and Ellen Davidson, *Open Minds to Equality*, 2nd ed. Allyn and Bacon, Needham Heights, MA. © 1998.

Teaching Tolerance, a publication of the Southern Poverty Law Center. Fall 1997 (Grade 5); Spring 1999 (Grade 1).

Weiss, Evelyn, ed., Priscilla Prutzman, Nancy Silber, *Children's Songs for a Friendly Planet*. World Around Songs, Inc., 1986.

York, Stacey, *Roots & Wings: Affirming Culture in Early Childhood Programs*. Redleaf Press / a division of Resources for Child Caring, St. Paul, MN. 1991.

Index Activities Closings Gatherings Charts Handouts Webs

Activities

Additional Activities

Closings

Gatherings

Handouts, Charts and Webs